# LET'S LEARN ABOUT...
# THE OCEAN

### Teacher's Guide
### CBeebies

# K1

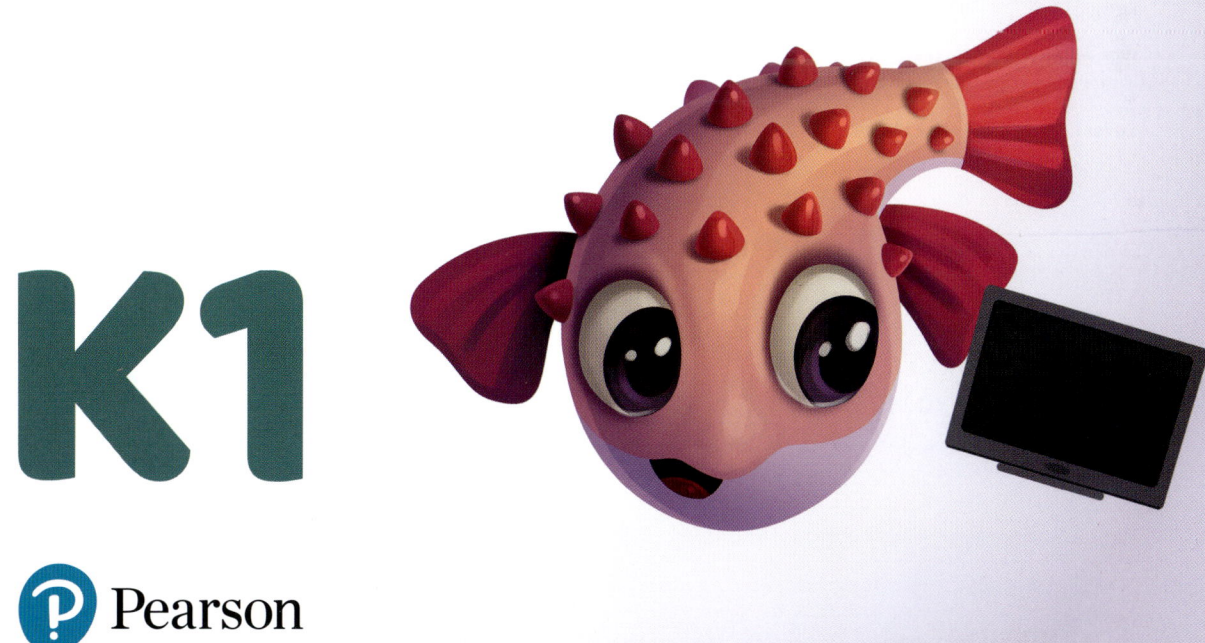

**Pearson**

**Pearson Education Limited**
KAO Two, KAO Park, Harlow, Essex, CM17 9NA, England
and Associated Companies around the world.

© Pearson Education Limited 2020

The right of Rhiannon S. Ball to be identified as author of this Work has been asserted by them in accordance with the Copyright, Designs and Patents Act 1988.

All rights reserved; no part of this publication may be reproduced, stored in a retrieval system, or transmitted in any form or by any means, electronic, mechanical, photocopying, recording, or otherwise without the prior written permission of the Publishers.

First published 2020

ISBN: 978-1-292-33456-1

Set in Mundo Sans
Printed in China (SWTC/01)

**Acknowledgements**
The publishers and author(s) would like to thank the following people and institutions for their feedback and comments during the development of the material: Marcos Mendonça, Leandra Dias, Viviane Kirmeliene, Simara H. Dal'Alba, Mônica Bicalho and GB Editorial. The publishers would also like to thank all the teachers who contributed to the development of *Let's learn about...*: Adriano de Paula Souza, Aline Ramos Teixeira Santo, Aline Vitor Rodrigues Pina Pereira, Ana Paula Gomez Montero, Anna Flávia Feitosa Passos, Camila Jarola, Celiane Junker Silva, Edegar França Junior, Fabiana Reis Yoshio, Fernanda de Souza Thomaz, Luana da Silva, Michael Iacovino Luidvinavicius, Munique Dias de Melo, Priscila Rossatti Duval Ferreira Neves, Sandra Ferito, and schools that took part in Construindo Juntos.

**Author Acknowledgements**
Rhiannon S. Ball

**Image Credit(s):**
**BBC Worldwide Learning:** 6, 6, 6, 10, 14, 16, 18, 14, 24, 28, 32, 34, 36, 38, 40, 42, 46, 52, 54, 56, 60, 64, 68; **Pearson Education Ltd:** Silva Serviços de Educação 12, 16, 16, 20, 26, 26, 26, 26, 26, 30, 32, 38, 38, 38, 38, 40, 40, 40, 40, 40, 44, 48, 48, 48, 48, 48, 48, 50, 50, 50, 60, 60, 60, 60, 66, 70; **Shutterstock.com:** BudOlga 8, Moomchak V. Design 8, Puslatronik 8

**Illustration Acknowledgements**
Illustrated by Filipe Laurentino and Silva Serviços de Educação

**Cover illustration** © Filipe Laurentino

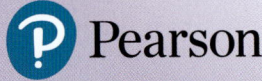

# Contents

| | Table of contents | 4 |
| | Presentation | 6 |
| U1 | How are we all similar? | 8 |
| U2 | How are we all different? | 16 |
| U3 | What is a family? | 24 |
| U4 | Do you share your toys? | 32 |
| U5 | How do you help at home? | 40 |
| U6 | How do you take care of pets? | 48 |
| U7 | What's your favorite food? | 56 |
| U8 | What do you like about school? | 64 |

# Table of contents - CBeebies

| UNIT | LESSON 1 | LESSON 2 | LESSON 3 | LESSON 4 |
|---|---|---|---|---|
| **Unit 1**<br>How are we all similar?<br>page 8 | • Understand what a shadow is<br>• Identify their own shadow and animal shadows<br>• Understand familiar words in a video | • Identify and name parts of the face<br>• Identify differences in size of parts of the face<br>• Understand familiar words in a video | • Understand what a shadow is<br>• Cognitive skills development in context<br>• Watch and follow a story in a video | • Understand what a shadow is<br>• Cognitive and motor skills development in context<br>• Explain understanding of a video |
| **Unit 2**<br>How are we all different?<br>page 16 | • Classify objects as big or small<br>• Make choices independently and as part of a group<br>• Understand familiar words in a video | • Develop creative and motor skills<br>• Understand, distinguish, and name parts of the body<br>• Use visuals to understand a video | • Develop creative and motor skills in context<br>• Understand instructions (rules)<br>• Watch and follow a story in a video | • Develop creative and motor skills in context<br>• Understand instructions<br>• Understand an animated video |
| **Unit 3**<br>What is a family?<br>page 24 | • Develop fine motor skills to make a rainbow<br>• Identify, name, and compare different shapes and colors<br>• Understand familiar words in a video | • Count one to five<br>• Recognize numbers one to five<br>• Understand familiar words in a video | • Count to five<br>• Develop cognitive and motor skills<br>• Use visuals to understand a video | • Develop fine motor skills in context<br>• Practice words for family members<br>• Understand familiar words in a video |
| **Unit 4**<br>Do you share your toys?<br>page 32 | • Count and identify different balls of different sizes<br>• Talk about toys, commands, and rules<br>• Understand familiar words in a video | • Develop creative and imaginative skills<br>• Talk about toys, commands, and rules<br>• Understand familiar words in a video | • Count to five<br>• Recognize numbers and develop motor skills<br>• Watch and follow a story in a video | • Develop cognitive and motor skills in context<br>• Talk about toys, commands, and rules<br>• Understand an animated video |

| UNIT | LESSON 1 | LESSON 2 | LESSON 3 | LESSON 4 |
|---|---|---|---|---|
| **Unit 5**<br>How do you help at home?<br>page 40 | • Practice saying colors and numbers in context<br>• Talk about different houses and things around them<br>• Understand familiar words in a video | • Talk about different houses and places in the house<br>• Understand what a lighthouse is<br>• Explain understanding of a video | • Identify what is in the kitchen<br>• Talk about different houses and places in the house<br>• Understand familiar words in a video | • Develop motor skills and creativity<br>• Talk about different houses and places in the house<br>• Give their opinion on a video |
| **Unit 6**<br>How do you take care of your pet?<br>page 48 | • Associate animals with their habitats<br>• Practice using words for body parts and size in context<br>• Use visuals to understand a video | • Count to seven<br>• Develop motor skills in context<br>• Understand familiar words in a video | • Count to seven<br>• Identify and classify animals<br>• Understand familiar words in a video | • Recognize what a dog needs<br>• Understand that pets have needs and we need to take care of them<br>• Explain understanding of a video |
| **Unit 7**<br>What is your favorite food?<br>page 56 | • Learn about different types of food<br>• Understand about what a fruit is<br>• Understand familiar words in a video | • Express preference about fruits<br>• Learn about different types of food<br>• Give their opinion on a video | • Count to nine<br>• Develop motor skills in context<br>• Understand familiar words in a video | • Learn and practice words for farm food<br>• Understand a story about food<br>• Explain understanding of a story in a video |
| **Unit 8**<br>What do you like about school?<br>page 64 | • Develop creative and motor skills in context<br>• Learn about classroom objects<br>• Use visuals to understand a video | • Count to ten<br>• Recognize numbers up to ten in context<br>• Understand familiar words in a video | • Count to ten<br>• Develop creative and motor skills in context<br>• Understand familiar words in a video | • Ask and answer what and where something is<br>• Recognize prepositions of place<br>• Explain understanding of a video |

# Presentation

*Let's Learn About...* is a bilingual program which aims to develop a wide variety of skills and knowledge of different subjects. To this end, several additional components ensure that students work on creative learning, pre-coding, *STEAM* lessons, personal, social, and emotional development, and much more. Teachers can find a complete mapping of the components online and suggested weekly planning to help them make the most of our interdisciplinary approach. All of the components in the program provide students with the opportunity to build a solid foundation and prepare themselves for the challenges ahead. The lessons help children explore and learn more about the world around them. The *CBeebies Project Book* introduces videos as a fun, educational tool for the pre-school classroom.

## Learning principles behind the CBeebies component

*CBeebies* is a British television channel that is owned by the BBC. It produces and broadcasts content for children aged below six.

Pre-school children are considered the digital generation; they do not know a life without screens and technology. Although excessive screen time is not advised for children in this age group, controlled access to quality content can aid students' development. In *Let's Learn About...* screen time is not a passive, individual activity; on the contrary, students are invited to share the watching experience together, with the well-planned interruptions from the teacher to highlight important language and plot developments to speed up students' language acquisition and work on creative and critical thinking skills.

The *CBeebies* videos used in *Let's Learn About...* have been carefully curated by education specialists at the BBC to ensure that they match students' learning needs and developmental abilities. The videos contain episodes of popular *CBeebies* TV shows, including both animated cartoons and documentary-style programs. They offer students contact with authentic content, featuring speakers with different accents and speaking at a natural pace. Students aren't expected to understand everything, but will gradually begin to pick up the language.

Familiarity is important for learning at this age and involving characters in learning material can help with this. In each volume of *CBeebies*, students will watch several episodes of each TV show, helping them grow a love for the characters, which in turn increases motivation and excitement about the lessons.

## How to work with the CBeebies Project Book

All *Let's learn about...* Project Books may have their pages removed. Before starting an activity in their Project Books, students can be instructed to take out the page they are going to work on and add it to a folder of their choice, so that students' work can be shared with parents regularly. This page, together with the projects students have developed in other project lessons, can become part of a portfolio created alongside with the teacher.

The aim of a portfolio is to show the cumulative efforts and progress students have made over time. This is also a great way to evaluate their improvement in all learning areas and the mastery of several skills. Students should be encouraged to share the work in their portfolio with their parents so that they can support their child's learning and be an active part of their development as a student. An assessment chart is available in the Extra Resources folder at Pearson English Portal for teachers to print and fill out with students' performance and attached to the portfolio folder.

**Kit and Pup**

**Nelly and Nora**

**Yakka Dee**

# What's in a *CBeebies* lesson?

*CBeebies* lessons follow similar routines to the ones that students develop in all the *Let's Learn About...* components, including the visual schedule, attention-getters, and *hello* and *goodbye* songs and routines.

In each lesson, students do a *before watching*, *while watching*, and *after watching* activity related to an episode of a *CBeebies* TV show. The *before watching* activity aims at introducing and practicing key language that will appear in the video; the *while watching* video is the moment when students watch the video with the teacher, during which guidance is given on specific moments to pause the video to ask questions, check students' understanding, etc.; and the *after watching* activity gives students the opportunity to reflect on the video further through a Project Book, craft, or role-play activity.

For each unit, there are two CLIL videos and one story time video; therefore, one video is watched over two lessons, giving students the opportunity to re-watch enjoyable content (something that children in this age group love to do!) and then reflect on it from a different angle. The story time videos feature an episode from the following TV shows: *Nelly and Nora* (Volume 1), *Sarah and Duck* (Volume 2), *Go Jetters* (Volume 3). Before you show these videos, we suggest that you say to students, *We're going to watch another episode of (Nelly and Nora). What is (Nelly) like? And (Nora)? Do you remember what happened in the last episode? What do you think happens today?* You can do this in a mixture of L1 and English or only in L1, according to your students' abilities.

There are two Project Book pages per unit instead of one per lesson, which adds variety to classes and keeps students motivated. The other two lessons per unit involve a mixture of games, craft making, singing, and drawing activities, which provide an important contrast to the video time activity, during which students should be reminded to sit still and watch quietly.

# Components

### For teachers
- *CBeebies* Teacher's Guide
- Video library with *CBeebies* videos available at Pearson English Portal
- Audio library with songs available at Pearson English Portal

### For students
- *CBeebies* Project Book with stickers

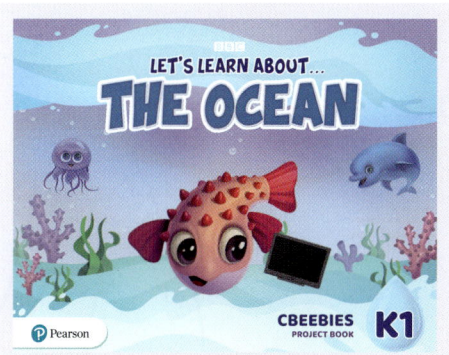

# Taking it further

If you notice that your students are developing a love for the characters featured in the *CBeebies* videos, you may like to access the official websites for these shows and download the additional resources–such as coloring pages and craft activities-featuring the characters for students to work on at home or during a rainy-day recess. The *CBeebies* official website also contains additional activities and useful articles.

**CBeebies**
https://global.cbeebies.com/
https://global.cbeebies.com/grown-ups/ (for educators and parents)

**Go Jetters**
https://www.gojetters.com/

**Sarah and Duck**
https://www.sarahandduck.com/

**Yakka Dee**
http://yakkadee.com/
[All links accessed on October 22, 2019]

Presentation 7

# Unit 1 How are we similar?

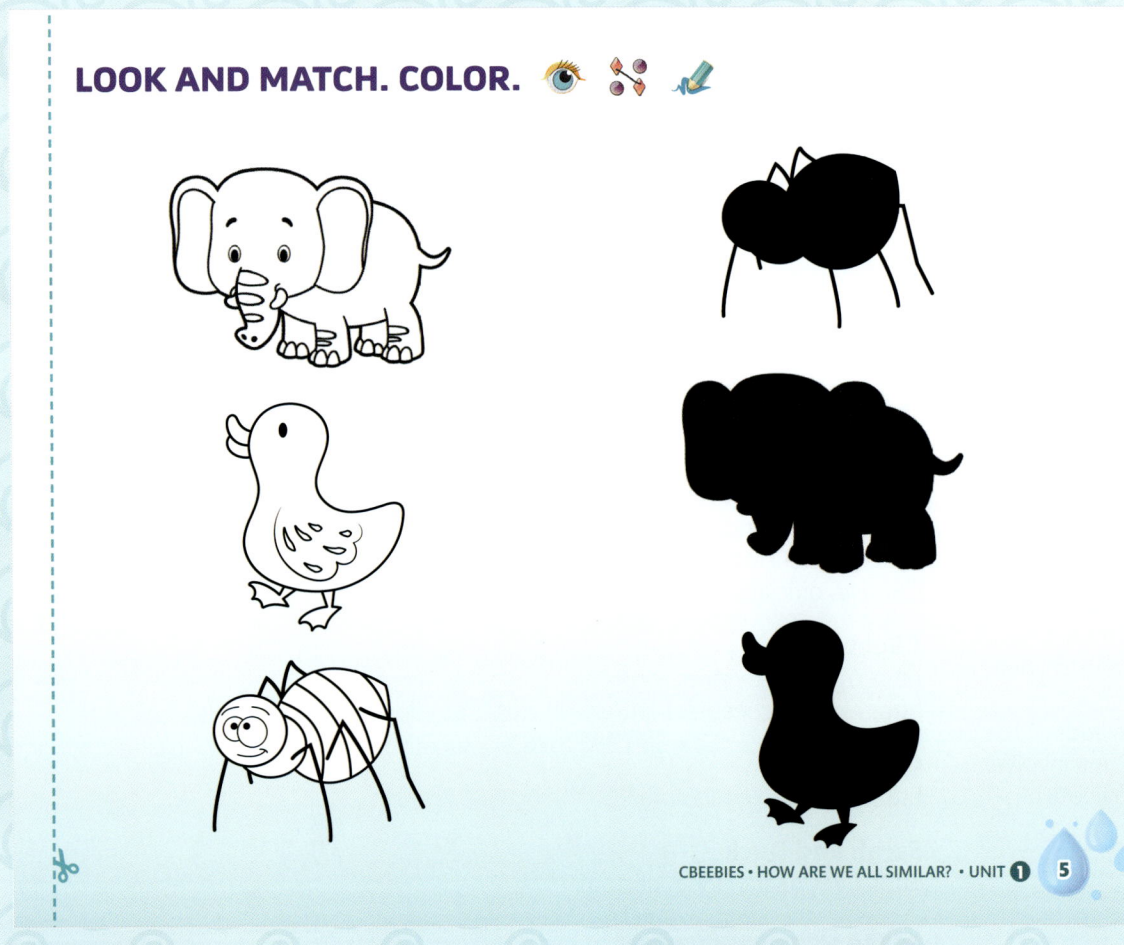

### Learning goals
- Understand what a shadow is
- Identify their own shadow and animal shadows
- Understand familiar words in a video

### Main language content
Animals: *duck, elephant, spider*
*How are you? I'm (fine/happy).*
*Hello shadow! Oh look... Let's... Can you find your shadow? Whose shadow is it? It's my shadow. It's your shadow.*

## OPENING

### Circle time

**Materials and preparation**
- Puppet
- Soft ball
- Visual schedule pictures

Take the soft ball, say, *hello*, and pass it round the circle. Encourage students to say, *hello* as they pass the ball to each other. Sit down together in the circle. Introduce the puppet and together say, *hello*. Ask the puppet, *How are you?* The puppet says, *I'm fine*. Mime thumbs up and say, *I'm fine*. Ask the puppet again and the puppet answers, *I'm happy*. Mime a big smile and a thumbs up. The puppet asks the class, *How are you?* Mime and say, *I'm fine* and *I'm happy*.

> **Note to teachers**
> The first circle time will take time to organize. Don't force students to respond / repeat phrases at this stage. Encourage students who do the actions and participate without saying the words.

Teach students the opening attention-getter:
**T:** *Come and sit close to me. It's time for...*
**S:** *CBeebies!*
Or
**T:** *1, 2, 3! It's time for...*
**S:** *CBeebies!*
Explain to students that whenever you use an attention-getter, they should stop talking and look at you.
Have students sit in a circle. Show students the visual schedule pictures. Ask for volunteers to help you turn them over. Encourage the whole class to say what each picture shows. Ask students to help you select the pictures that show today's schedule as you tell them what they are going to do today.

**Play *Musical statues*.**

### Materials and preparation
- Audio library – songs

Stand together in a circle and play a song. Dance together in the circle. Stop the music and everybody freezes. Play the music again and say, *Let's dance together.* When you stop the music say, *Statues!* and everybody freezes one more time.

# ACTIVE LEARNING

### Before watching the video - Animal shadows

### Materials and preparation
- A lamp
- Silhouettes of a spider, elephant, and duck (cut out A4 size from black construction paper)

If possible, use sunlight or the classroom lights to show students your shadow. Show your shadow moving. Invite students to try to find, chase, and catch their shadow. Show students the silhouettes and say the names of the animals. Put the lamp in front of the class so every student can see. Show students the shadow of each animal. Show students how to use their hands, arms, and body to make a spider, duck, and elephant. You can follow the script below when talking to students:
*Look - it's my shadow. Hello shadow. Oh look - my shadow moves! It's my shadow. Can you find your shadow? Let's try. Oh look - it's your shadow. Hello shadow. Whose shadow is it? It's a duck/elephant/spider. Let's make a spider shadow - like this. Use your hands.*

> **Note to teachers**
> Students may find it challenging to use their hands and arms as they are still developing motor skills. Don't expect students to say or remember the animal words - these are not important at this stage.

### Watching the video - Let's watch!

### Materials and preparation
- Video Library

Sit together in a semicircle and make sure every student can see the screen properly. Say, *Let's watch together. Show me, show me shadows! Hello shadows!* Play the video *Show me, show me*, Series 2 Ep. 23, *Moon & Shadows* (video 1), and watch it together. Watch the video again and stop the clip each time a child makes the spider, the duck, and the elephant. Ask students to make the shapes with your hands, arm, and body.

### After watching the video – Look and match. Color.

### Materials and preparation
- Project Book page 5
- Crayons
- Pencils

Help students open their Project Books to page 5. Point to the spider, duck, and elephant and practice the words with students. Give students a pencil each and tell them to find and match the animals with their shadows. Students can then color the animals.

> **Note to teachers**
> Students will need time and support. Allow enough time and focus students on one animal at a time. Playing a song or singing together will keep students on track.

# DIFFERENTIATED INSTRUCTION

### BELOW LEVEL
### Before watching the video
Focus on just the spider to try and make a shadow, working on motor-skills and connecting movement and shadows.

### ABOVE LEVEL
### Before watching the video
Students mingle and freeze, looking and saying, *your shadow, my shadow*. Extend by getting students to play with light and their hands creating different shadow shapes.

# CLOSING

### Get ready to leave. Sing the *Goodbye song*.

### Materials and preparation
- Audio library – songs

Show and help put their things away and get ready to leave.
Sing the *Goodbye song* (track 5) and invite students to sing along. Say *goodbye* to students and have them say *goodbye* back to you. Say *goodbye* to your shadow.

### Learning goals
- Identify and name parts of the face
- Identify differences in size of parts of the face
- Understand familiar words in a video

### Main language content
*How are you?*
*I'm... fine, happy, sad, tired*
Parts of the body: *ears, eyes, mouth, nose, face*
*my nose, your nose*
*It's long/little.*
*Let's scratch/sniff/sneeze/blow/snore*

# OPENING

**Circle time**

**Materials and preparation**
- Puppet
- Soft ball
- Video schedule pictures

Take the soft ball, say, *hello*, and pass it round the circle. Students say *hello* as they pass it on. Sit down together in the circle. Say *hello* to the puppet and ask, *How are you?* The puppet says, *I'm fine, happy, sad,* and *tired.* Mime each feeling together. Encourage students to ask each other how they are.

> **Note to teachers**
> Allow students to express "negative" feelings, too—we can't expect them to always be fine and happy. It's important to let them express their real feelings.

Remind students of the opening attention-getter:
**T:** *Come and sit close to me. It's time for...*
**S:** *CBeebies!*
Or
**T:** *1, 2, 3! It's time for...*
**S:** *CBeebies!*
Explain to students that whenever you use an attention-getter, they should stop talking and look at you.
Have students sit in a circle. Show students the visual schedule pictures. Ask for volunteers to help you turn them over. Encourage the whole class to say what each picture shows. Ask students to help you select the pictures that show today's schedule as you tell them what they are going to do today.

**Play *Musical chairs*.**

**Materials and preparation**
- Audio library – songs

Put the classroom chairs in a circle. Play the music and when it stops, everybody sits down. Repeat this a few times so students get the idea. Take away a chair and play the music. When it stops students have to try to find a seat.

## ACTIVE LEARNING

### Before watching the video - My face
**Materials and preparation**
- Flashcards: ears, eyes, mouth, nose, face

Slow reveal each of the flashcards and say the name. Encourage students to point to their parts of the face as you show the flashcards. Stick the flashcards around the room. Stand together in the center, call out a face word, and students run to the card. Sit together in a circle and show the nose card. Mime *scratch*, *sniff*, *blow*, *sneeze*, and *snore*. Encourage students to copy you and say the word. Call out an action for students to mime.

> **Note to teachers**
> This activity will help with recognition and cement meaning and understanding. Don't worry if students can't say each word.

### Watching the video - Let's watch!
**Materials and preparation**
- Video Library

Sit together in a circle so everyone can see the screen. Watch the video together. Watch it again and stop when Yakka Dee says, *my nose / your nose* and students say and point. Continue the video and then pause again to mime *little* and *long nose*. Continue the video and pause it to do the actions *sniff*, *blow*, and *snore* together. You should set expectations of correct watching behavior, reminding students that they should sit still and watch quietly, respecting their classmates.

### After watching the video – Make a face mask.
**Materials and preparation**
- Colored markers
- Elastic
- Nose shapes (different shapes and sizes) cut out of construction paper
- Paper plates

Sit students at their tables and give each student a paper plate. Students look, listen, and point to the different parts of their faces as you say the words. Mime a little and a long nose and ask students to choose which one they want for their face. Students stick on their choice of nose. Students color the face. Attach elastic to the paper plates so students to wear the mask.

> **Note to teachers**
> Allow students to select freely which nose and the colors to use for the face. This is important for creative and imaginative development.

## DIFFERENTIATED INSTRUCTION

### BELOW LEVEL
**Before watching the video**
Focus on fewer parts of the face during the flashcard game of recognition - just eyes and ears. Play *Touch your (eyes/nose)* to reinforce meaning; you give the command and students touch the correct body part.

### ABOVE LEVEL
**After watching the video**
Allow students to select little or long ears, cut them out of paper, and stick on the sides of the face mask. Get students to mingle with their face masks on and encourage students to say, *My nose is little / long* and *Your nose is little / long*. Extend to include ears.

## CLOSING

### Goodbye, nose. Sing the *Goodbye song*.
**Materials and preparation**
- Audio library – songs

Students put on/hold their face mask and say goodbye to their little or long noses. Sing the *Goodbye* song (track 5) and invite students to sing along. Say *goodbye* to them and have them say *goodbye* back to you. Play the video *Yakka Dee, Series 2, Ep. 6, Nose* (video 2), and watch it together.

**LOOK, THINK, AND DRAW.**

**Learning goals**
- Understand what a shadow is
- Develop cognitive skills in context
- Watch and follow a story in a video

**Main language content**
At the beach: *beach, sand, bucket, spade, sandcastle, sun, shell*
*The sun makes a shadow.*

# OPENING

### Circle time

**Materials and preparation**
- Audio library – songs
- Puppet
- Soft ball
- Visual schedule pictures

Stand together in a circle and sing the *Hello song* (track 4). Take the soft ball, say, *hello*, and pass it round the circle. Students say *hello* as they pass it on. Sit down together in the circle. Say, *hello* to the puppet and ask, *How are you?* The puppet says, *I'm fine, happy, sad,* and *tired*. Mime each feeling together. Encourage students to ask each other how they are.

> **Note to teachers**
> Don't force students to respond/repeat phrases at this stage. Encourage students who do the actions and participate without saying the words.

Have students sit in a circle. Show students the visual schedule pictures. Ask for volunteers to help you turn them over. Encourage the whole class to say what each picture shows. Ask students to help you select the pictures that show today's schedule as you tell them what they are going to do today.

### Shadow theater

**Materials and preparation**
- A cardboard box
- A low table
- Lamp or flashlight
- Tissue paper

Cut a hole in the front of the cardboard box and stick the tissue paper on the inside to cover the hole. Place the box on a low table and shine the lamp or flashlight behind the box so the light is in the center of the tissue paper. Sit students in a semicircle so everyone can see the box. Use your hand/s to make different shadows and shadow movements. Invite students to come behind the table to try out making different shadows for the rest of the class to see.

# ACTIVE LEARNING

### Before watching the video – At the beach

### Materials and preparation
- Printouts: beach, sea, bucket, spade, sandcastle, shell, sun
- flyswatters x 2

Sit together in a circle. Slowly reveal each of the printouts. Mix the printouts up in front of the circle. Call out a word, give students the flyswatter, and students find and swat the correct word. Have students pass around the flyswatter so everyone has a turn.

> **Note to teachers**
> Ask students about their vacation and if they like to play on the beach and make sandcastles.

### Watching the video
### Materials and preparation
- Video library

Sit together in a semicircle and make sure all students can see. Play the video *Nelly & Nora, Ep. 45, The shadow castle* (video 3), and watch it together. Watch the video again and stop at objects in the video and ask students what they are. Stop and ask students what happens to Nora's castle. Ask students what kind of castle Nelly and Nora want to build.

You should set expectations of correct watching behavior, reminding students that they should sit still and watch quietly, respecting their classmates.

### After watching the video – Look, think, and draw.

### Materials and preparation
- Colored pencils
- Pencils
- Project Book page 7

Sit students at their tables. Help students open their Project Books to page 7. Point to the sandcastle, sun, and shadow. Show students how to trace the sandcastle shadow. Highlight the position of the sun behind the sandcastle. Put the colored pencils in the center of the tables and give students a pencil each. Invite students to trace the sandcastle shadow. Then ask, *What color do you need for the shadow?* and help them identify the black pencil. They color in the shadow.

> **Note to teachers**
> Fast finishers can color the sun and the castle. Then they decorate the castle by drawing on shells.

# DIFFERENTIATED INSTRUCTION

### BELOW LEVEL
### Before watching the video
Focus on only *sandcastle*, *sun*, and *bucket* to introduce the key video concept and language. Mime using a bucket to build a sandcastle and pretending to be the sun casting a shadow.

### ABOVE LEVEL
### After watching the video
Invite students to draw a crab on top of the castle in their Project Books and then draw the crab's shadow.

# CLOSING

### Show and tell. Sing the *Goodbye song*.

### Materials and preparation
- Audio library – songs

Have students sit in a circle and show each other their pictures. Encourage them to show what they have drawn.
Sing the *Goodbye song* (track 5) and invite students to sing along. Say *goodbye* to them and have them say *goodbye* back to you.

**Learning goals**
- Understand what a shadow is
- Develop cognitive and motor skills in context
- Explain understanding of a video

**Main language content**
At the beach: *at the beach, sandcastle, bucket, spade, crab, shell, sun*
*The sun makes a shadow.*

# OPENING

### Circle time

**Materials and preparation**
- Audio library – songs
- Puppet
- Soft ball
- Visual schedule pictures

Stand together in a circle and sing the *Hello song* (track 4). Take the soft ball, say, *hello*, and pass it round the circle. Students say, *hello* as they pass it on. Sit down together in the circle. Say *hello* to the puppet and ask, *How are you?* The puppet says *I'm fine, happy, sad,* and *tired.* Mime each feeling together. Encourage students to ask each other how they are.

> **Note to teachers**
> Allow students to express "negative" feelings, too - we can't expect them to always be fine and happy. It's important to let them express their real feelings.

Have students sit in a circle. Show students the visual schedule pictures. Ask for volunteers to help you turn them over. Encourage the whole class to say what each picture shows. Ask students to help you select the pictures that show today's schedule as you tell them what they are going to do today.

### At the beach

**Materials and preparation**
- A bucket and spade
- Sandbox (optional)

Stick the flashcards on the board. Say, *We're going to the beach!* Mime being at the beach, using a spade in the sand, filling a bucket, and making a sandcastle. Mime being the sun shining down on the beach and the sandcastle. Mime being crabs, walking sideways, and climbing in and out of a shell. Encourage students to join in; offer them the props so they can act out for their classmates to guess what they are doing.

### Note to teachers
If possible, bring in a sandbox and invite students to make sandcastles. They could even have a sandcastle competition and describe the sandcastles using *big* and *small*.

## ACTIVE LEARNING

### Before watching the video – Say the words.

#### Materials and preparation
- Printouts: beach, sandcastle, bucket, spade, crab, shell, sun

Sit together in a circle. Slowly reveal each of the printouts. Pass a picture to the left and a different picture to the right, and invite students to say the word. Continue giving the pictures to the left and to the right for students to say the words and pass the printout on.

### Note to teachers
This will be noisy as everyone should be saying the word as they receive the card. By allowing everyone to speak students will build confidence and it will feel less pressurized than speaking in front of the whole class.

### Watching the video – Let's watch!
#### Materials and preparation
- Video library

Sit together in a semicircle and make sure everyone can see. Play the video *Nelly & Nora, Ep. 45, The shadow castle* (video 3), and watch it together. Pause to say the familiar words with students. Stop and mime the actions in the story together. You should set expectations of correct watching behavior, reminding students that they should sit still and watch quietly, respecting their classmates.

### After watching the video – Make a crab.
#### Materials and preparation
- Colored markers
- Glue
- Paper plates
- Popsicle sticks
- Red construction paper (one sheet per student)
- Scissors
- Split pins

Sit students at their tables. Give students a paper plate each and a sheet of red construction paper. Ask students to draw two crab arms on the red card and cut them out. Show students how to attach the crab arms using split pins to the side of the paper plate. Students draw a face in the center of the paper plate and color the plate red. Stick a popsicle stick on the bottom of the paper plate for students to hold on to.

### Note to teachers
Students can stick the arms on the plate rather than using spilt pins.

## DIFFERENTIATED INSTRUCTION

### BELOW LEVEL
#### Before watching the video
If students are not yet ready to produce the language, stick the pictures up around the room and call out a word for students to find and run to.

### ABOVE LEVEL
#### After watching the video
Ask students what they can remember from the video and invite students to use the flashcards to retell/reconstruct the story before watching it. Encourage students to mime and act out the parts they can remember.

## CLOSING

### Crab race. Sing the *Goodbye song*.
#### Materials and preparation
- Audio library – songs

Invite students to sit in a circle. Call on two students and have the "race" their crabs down the circle.
Sing the *Goodbye song* (track 5) and invite students to sing along. Say *goodbye* to them and have them say *goodbye* back to you.

# Unit 2 How are we all different?

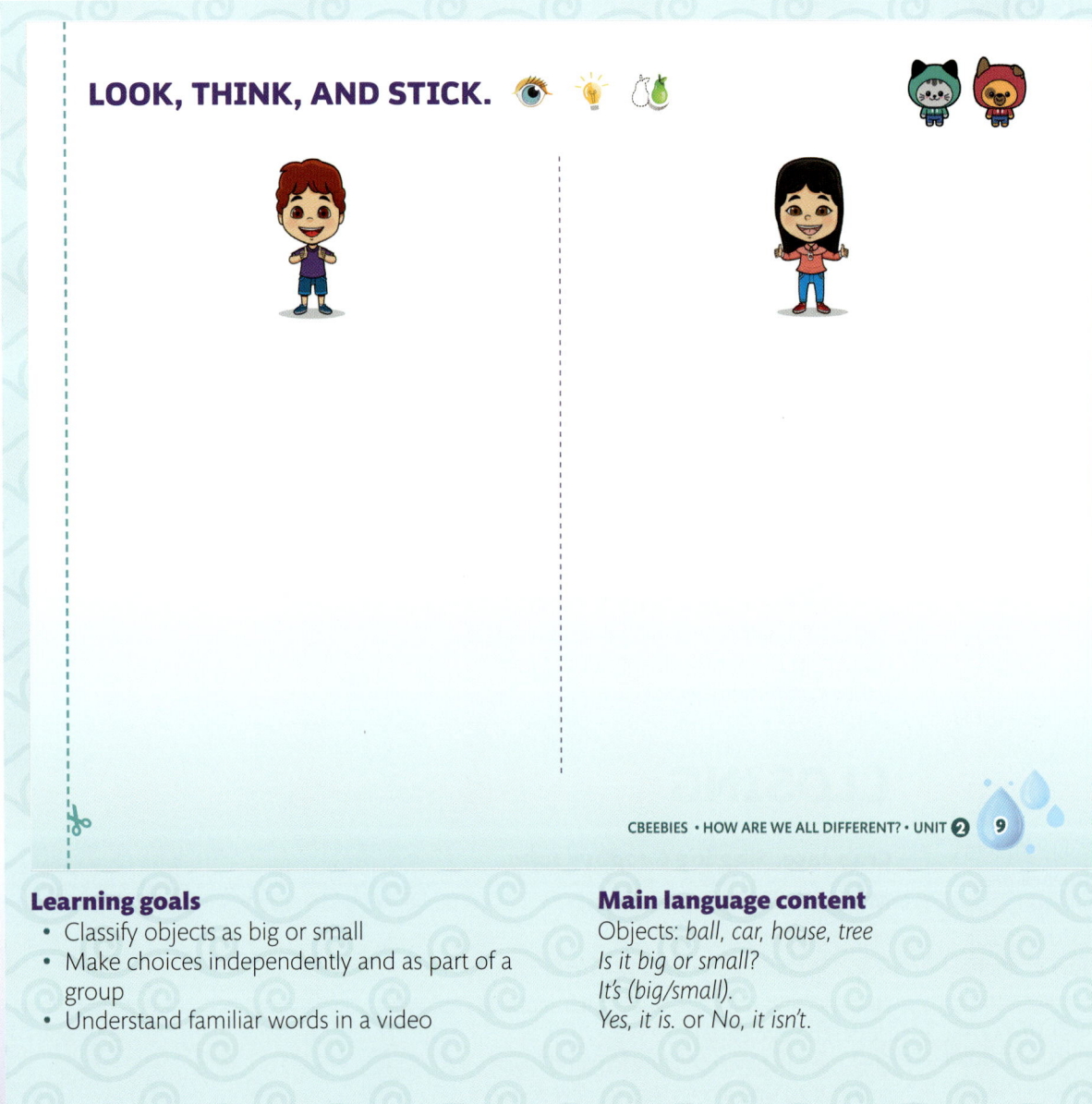

**Learning goals**
- Classify objects as big or small
- Make choices independently and as part of a group
- Understand familiar words in a video

**Main language content**
Objects: *ball, car, house, tree*
*Is it big or small?*
*It's (big/small).*
*Yes, it is.* or *No, it isn't.*

## OPENING

**Circle time**

**Materials and preparation**
- A soft ball
- Audio library – songs
- Puppet
- Visual schedule pictures

Sit together in a circle and sing the *Hello song* (track 4). Give students the soft ball to pass on to other students and say, *hello*. Say, *Hello, how are you?* to the puppet and encourage students to greet it with *hello* or *hi*.

> **Note to teachers**
> At this stage repetition and consistency is important for students. Allow students to mime their answers if they are not yet ready to answer.

Remind students of the opening attention-getter:
**T:** *Come and sit close to me. It's time for...*
**S:** *CBeebies!*
Or
**T:** *1, 2, 3! It's time for...*
**S:** *CBeebies!*
Explain to students that whenever you use an attention-getter, they should stop talking and look at you.
Have students sit in a circle. Show students the visual schedule pictures. Ask for volunteers to help you turn them over. Encourage the whole class to say what each picture shows. Ask students to help you select the pictures that show today's schedule as you tell them what they are going to do today.

> **Note to teachers**
> You can also teach/review the attention-getter *All set? You bet!*

### Big circle, small circle

Ask students to stand together in a circle holding hands and stretching out together to make a big circle, saying, *big, big circle*. Repeat with *small, small circle* and getting in close together. Repeat it several times. Stand together and ask students to make themselves *big* (reaching up and out). Now ask students to make themselves *small* (crouching down). Repeat several times.

## ACTIVE LEARNING

### Before watching the video – Is it big or small?

#### Materials and preparation

- A box
- Several balls of different sizes (alternatively you can use building blocks of different sizes)

In a circle, show students a ball, say, *ball*, and encourage them to repeat after you. Roll the ball to different students and ask them to roll it back to you. Take a different bigger ball and say, *big ball*; repeat with *small ball*. Put all the balls together in a box; pick out a big ball, and say, *big ball*. Repeat with *small ball*. Invite students to pick a ball from the box. Ask the class, *Is it big or small?* Elicit the answers *yes/no*.

#### Note to teachers

You can use building blocks if you can't get different size balls. Students don't have to repeat the full phrase – recognition of *big* and *small* is enough.

### Watching the video – Let's watch!

#### Materials and preparation

- Video library

Sit together and make sure everyone can see the screen/board. Play the video *Kit and Pup, Ep. 26, Big and small* (video 4), and watch it together. Then divide the class into two groups. One group is Kit and the other is Pup. Watch it again and pause when Kit & Pup first appear – each group gets their correct size ball (Pup's group gets the small ball and Kit's group gets the big ball). Continue watching until the end of the Kit vs. Pup game and stop. Ask the Pup's group to find big objects and the Kit's group to find small objects – count and see who wins.
You should set expectations of correct watching behavior, reminding students that they should sit still and watch quietly, respecting their classmates.

### After watching the video – Look, think, and stick.

#### Materials and preparation

- Project Book page 9

Help students open their Project Books to page 9. Point to the pictures of the children, and say, *big* and *small*. Mime in the same way as the pictures to help students' understanding and encourage them to mime and say the words. Help students to turn to the stickers page and find the stickers for Unit 2. Encourage students to identify where to stick each sticker in their Project Books. At this age, students usually struggle to peel off and stick the stickers correctly. Monitor and help as needed. Finally point to each sticker and ask students, *Is it big or small?* Encourage them to say, *It's big* or *It's a big house*.

#### Note to teachers

Do the activity together to help students complete the task. Students will probably struggle to follow long instructions, so a model works best.

## DIFFERENTIATED INSTRUCTION

### BELOW LEVEL
### Before watching the video

Focus on only one big ball and one small ball. Invite students to listen and point to correct ball as you call out the name.

### ABOVE LEVEL
### Before watching the video

#### Materials and preparation

- Boxes filled with balls, building blocks, toys, stuffed toys in different sizes (big and small)

Extend the activity by putting a box of balls, a box of building blocks, a box of toys, and a box of stuffed toys in different parts of the classroom. Divide the class into four groups and assign a box to each group. Each group works together to sort the things in the box into big and small. Move groups round to the next corner.

## CLOSING

### Point to big, point to small. Sing the Goodbye song.

#### Materials and preparation

- Audio library – songs

Have students walk around the classroom and point to big and small objects in the classroom as you say, *big* or *small*. Sing the *Goodbye song* (track 5) and invite students to sing along while they put their things away. Encourage students to help each other. Say *goodbye* to them and have them say *goodbye* back to you.

**Learning goals**
- Understand, distinguish, and name parts of the body
- Develop creative and motor skills
- Use visuals to understand a video

**Main language content**
Actions: *clap, shake, stamp, wave*
Animal: *butterfly*
Parts of the body: *arms, body, feet, hands, head, legs*
*Can you (clap)?*

# OPENING

**Circle time**

**Materials and preparation**
- A soft ball
- Puppet
- Visual schedule pictures

Say, *Hello, how are you?* to the puppet and encourage students to greet it with *hello* or *hi*. Have students sit in a circle. Roll the soft ball to a student and ask, *How are you?* Encourage them to answer (e.g. *I'm OK!*), roll the ball to a classmate, and ask them how they are. Repeat with other students as many times as possible.

> **Note to teachers**
> Encourage students to say how they are to as many classmates as possible to help create a learner-centered cooperative environment. Help them ask, *How are you?* by encouraging the class to ask in unison.

Remind students of the attention-getter and practice it with them:
**T:** *Come and sit close to me. It's time for…*
**S:** *CBeebies!*
Or
**T:** *1, 2, 3! It's time for…*
**S:** *CBeebies!*

> **Note to teachers**
> Remind students that they should be quiet and pay attention when you use the attention-getter.

Show them the visual schedule pictures. Choose a class helper of the day and have them order the pictures of the activities as they are mentioned.

**Move around.**

Ask students to stand together in a circle and put your hands out in front of you. Ask your students to do the same. Wave and then clap your hands; encourage students to do the same. Move around in a circle and wave then clap. Repeat with *stamp your feet shake your arms, shake your legs*, and *shake your body*. Stop and repeat from the beginning.
You should set expectations of walking safely to avoid accidents.

## ACTIVE LEARNING

**Before watching the video – Look and point.**

**Materials and preparation**
- Flashcards: *arms, body, feet, hands, head, legs*
- flyswatters (x2) (optional)

Ask students to sit in a circle. Reveal each flashcard slowly and put them in the center of the circle. Call out a body part and ask students to point to the correct flashcard. If you have the flyswatters, you can give them to two students and invite them to tap the correct flashcard. Then repeat with other students. Point to the hands and invite students to wave and clap. Point to the body and head, and invite students to shake. Point to the feet and invite students to stamp their feet.

**Note to teachers**

You can use the flyswatters to stop your students throwing themselves on the cards and to help them with physical and cognitive development.

**Watching the video – Let's watch!**

**Materials and preparation**
- Video library

Sit together so everyone can see the screen/board. Play the video *Show me, Show me, Series 6, Ep. 13, Winding and hands* (video 5), and watch it together. Ask students to show you the part of the body that is in the video. Ask students to show you what actions with hands they can remember from the video. Watch it again, pause it after each action of the hands and do it together.
You should set expectations of correct watching behavior, reminding students that they should sit still and watch quietly, respecting their classmates.

**After watching the video – Make a butterfly hand art.**

**Materials and preparation**
- Crayons (optional)
- Crepe paper (optional)
- Paint of different colors
- Paintbrushes
- Sheets of A3 paper (one per student)

Sit students at their table and give each one a sheet of A3 paper. Put the paint on the center of each table and give each student some paint (one or two colors). Students paint the palms of their hands and make a print of it on the paper, wrist to wrist together to make a butterfly shape. Students can then add details to finish the butterfly.

**Note to teachers**

If using paints is not possible, students can use crayons to draw around each hand, and then color and decorate the butterfly using crepe paper and other materials.

## DIFFERENTIATED INSTRUCTION

**BELOW LEVEL**
**Before watching the video**
Focus only on hands, then clap and wave. Stand in a circle and ask students to wave and then clap or high five each other.

**ABOVE LEVEL**
**Before watching the video**
Ask students to try and wave their feet, their body, and their head. Continue with other actions and body parts, asking students, *Can you (stamp) your (hands)?* Encourage them answer *yes/no*.

## CLOSING

**Show and tell. Sing the *Goodbye song*.**

**Materials and preparation**
- Audio library – songs
- Students' butterflies (from the previous activity)

Invite students to show their butterflies to their classmates, encouraging them to explain the shapes and colors. Sing the *Goodbye song* (track 5) and invite students to sing along. Say *goodbye* to them and have them say *goodbye* back to you.

**FIND AND CIRCLE. COUNT.**

CBEEBIES • HOW ARE WE ALL DIFFERENT? • UNIT 2   11

**Learning goals**
- Develop creative and motor skills in context
- Understand instructions (rules)
- Watch and follow a story in a video

**Main language content**
Animal: *sheep*
Game: *hide-and-seek.*
Weather: *could, cloudy, sun, sunny*
*I'm ready. I'm going to find you. I found you.*

# OPENING

## Circle time

**Materials and preparation**
- A soft ball
- Audio library – songs
- Puppet
- Visual schedule pictures

Stand together in a circle and sing the *Hello song* (track 4). Give students the soft ball to pass on to other students and say, *hello*. Say, *Hello, how are you?* to the puppet and encourage students to greet it with *hello* or *hi*.

> **Note to teachers**
> Encourage students to greet as many classmates as possible to help create a learner-centered, cooperative environment.

Remind students of the attention-getter and practice it with them:
**T:** *Come and sit close to me. It's time for…*
**S:** *CBeebies!*
Or
**T:** *1, 2, 3! It's time for…*
**S:** *CBeebies!*

> **Note to teachers**
> You can also teach/review the attention-getter *All set? You bet!*

Have students sit in a circle. Show each visual schedule pictures and then separate the ones that show the activities of today's class. Have a volunteer place the activities in the center of the circle.

## Play *Hide-and-seek.*

Take students outside or make space in the classroom. Divide the class into two groups. Ask one group to stand at the front facing the wall, while the other group hides around the class. Switch groups around so every student has the chance to hide and then seek.

20  CBeebies

> **Note to teachers**
> Feed-in and model appropriate language for the game, e.g.: *Let's play hide-and-seek, I'm ready, I'm going to find you, I found you.*

## ACTIVE LEARNING

### Before watching the video – What's the weather like?

#### Materials and preparation
- Printouts of a big sun and a big cloud
- Sticky tape

Sit together in a circle. Show students the big sun picture and together say, *It's sunny.* Stick the sun on the board. Show students the big cloud picture and together say, *It's cloudy.* Stick the cloud over the sun and then remove it. Divide the class into two groups. One group is the *sun* and the other group are the *clouds*. Act out *sunny* and *cloudy* by encouraging the "sunny" group to stand in front of the "cloudy" group and vice versa.

### Watching the video – Let's watch!

#### Materials and preparation
- Video library

Sit together and make sure all students can see the screen/board. Play the video *Nelly & Nora, Ep. 7, Hide and sheep* (video 6), and watch it together. Pause and say, *It's sunny* and *It's cloudy* with Nelly and Nora. Stop and point out the sheep playing hide-and-seek together; ask students to say where they are hiding.

### After watching the video – Find and circle. Count.

#### Materials and preparation
- Crayons
- Pencils
- Project Book page 11

Help students open their Project Books to page 11. Ask, *What can you see?* Give students a pencil each and put the crayons in the center of the table. Invite students to find and circle the sheep. Then invite them to count the sheep.
You should set expectations of correct watching behavior, reminding students that they should sit still and watch quietly, respecting their classmates.

## DIFFERENTIATED INSTRUCTION

### BELOW LEVEL
**Play *Hide-and-seek*.**
Use the puppet to introduce the game and introduce some of the language for the game, for example, have the puppet count to three and then say, *Ready or not...here I come!*

### ABOVE LEVEL
**After watching the video**
Invite students to describe where the sheep are hiding. Help students with prepositions of place and supporting language.

## CLOSING

### Listen and run. Sing the *Goodbye song*.

#### Materials and preparation
- Audio library – songs
- Printouts of a big sun and a big cloud
- Sticky tape

Stick the picture of the sun on a wall and the picture of the cloud to an opposite wall. Call out *sun* or *cloud* and have students run to one picture or another. You should set expectations of walking safely so as to avoid accidents.
Sing the *Goodbye song* (track 5) and invite students to sing along. Say *goodbye* to them and have them say *goodbye* back to you.

## Learning goals
- Develop creative and motor skills in context
- Understand instructions
- Understand an animated video

## Main language content
Animal: *sheep*
Game: *hide-and-seek, hot and cold*
Weather: *could, cloudy, sun, sunny*
*I'm ready. I'm going to find you. I found you.*

# OPENING

### Circle time

**Materials and preparation**
- Puppet
- Visual schedule pictures (hide them around the classroom)

Say, *Hello, how are you?* to the puppet and encourage students to greet it with *hello* or *hi*. Ask, *How are you?* Encourage them to answer (e.g. *I'm OK!*) and ask a classmate how they are.

Remind students of the attention-getter and practice it with them:
**T:** *Come and sit close to me. It's time for…*
**S:** *CBeebies!*
Or
**T:** *1, 2, 3! It's time for…*
**S:** *CBeebies!*

> **Note to teachers**
> Remind students that they should be quiet and pay attention when you use the attention-getter.

Hide the visual schedule pictures that refer to today's activities. Tell students to look for them around the classroom. As they find a picture, tell them to hand it to you. Then talk to students about each of the moments of the class.

### Play *Hide and seek* with toys.

**Materials and preparation**
- Several toys

Divide the class into two groups. Give one group some toys to hide around the classroom, while the other group sits with their eyes closed. Then the group that hid the toys sits down while the other group looks for the toys. Encourage them to call out *hot* and *cold* depending on how near/far the group is to/from the toys. Depending on the size of the class and your learning objectives for your students, you can do this with smaller groups and more/less toys. Make sure groups switch roles.

## ACTIVE LEARNING

### Before watching the video – Look and say.

**Materials and preparation**

- Printouts of a big sun and a big cloud (from the previous lesson)

Sit together in a circle. Show students the sun and encourage them to say, *It's sunny*. Cover up the sun with your hands and ask, *What happened?* Encourage students to think about why we can't see the sun sometimes (you can use in L1 as necessary). Show students the picture of the cloud and encourage them to say, *It's cloudy*. Put the big cloud picture in the circle. Invite students to point to one of the pictures and say the correct sentence/word. Allow as many students as possible to try.

> **Note to teachers**
> Encourage students to think and act out what they do on sunny and cloudy days.

### Watching the video – Let's watch!

**Materials and preparation**

- Video library

Sit together and make sure all students can see the screen/board. Play the video *Nelly & Nora, Ep. 7, Hide and sheep* (video 6), and watch it together. Pause to say the words related to weather. Encourage students to repeat after you. Compare the shapes of the sheep and the cloud. Ask where Nelly and Nora are hiding.

You should set expectations of correct watching behavior, reminding students that they should sit still and watch quietly, respecting their classmates.

### After watching the video – Make a sheep in the field picture.

**Materials and preparation**

- Cotton balls
- Crayons
- Glue
- Green cardboard paper & crepe paper
- Scissors
- Sheets of A4 construction paper (one per student)

Ask students to go to their seats and give them the materials. Show students how to stick the cotton wool on the card to make a sheep. Show students how to stick on green paper to make the grass. Students make a sheep and a field, then they draw legs and a face for each sheep. Make each step together with the students. Monitor and help as needed.

> **Note to teachers**
> You can invite students to draw a sun and clouds.

## DIFFERENTIATED INSTRUCTION

### BELOW LEVEL
### After watching the video

**Materials and preparation**

- Sheets of green A4 paper (one per student)

Invite students to make one large sheep on a sheet of green A4 paper. To support students further, stick and shape the sheep together, step by step, and together draw legs and a face.

### ABOVE LEVEL
### After watching the video

Remind students about the previous unit and shadows. Invite students to think about and try to draw shadows for the sheep on their paper.

## CLOSING

### Talk about the videos. Sing the *Goodbye song*.

**Materials and preparation**

- Audio library – songs

Talk to students about the videos they watched in this unit. Ask, *Which was your favorite? Why?*
Sing the *Goodbye song* (track 5) and invite students to sing along. Say *goodbye* to them and have them say *goodbye* back to you.

# Unit 3 What is a family?

### Learning goals
- Develop fine motor skills to make a rainbow
- Identify, name, and compare different shapes and colors
- Understand familiar words in a video

### Main language content
Colors: *blue, green, orange, pink, purple, red, yellow*
*(It's a) rainbow.*

## OPENING

**Circle time**

**Materials and preparation**
- A soft ball
- Audio library – songs
- Puppet
- Visual schedule pictures

Stand together in a circle and sing the *Hello song* (track 4). Give students the soft ball to pass on to other students and say, *hello*. Say, *Hello, how are you?* to the puppet and encourage students to do the same.

> **Note to teachers**
> At this stage repetition and consistency is important for students. Allow students to mime their answers if they are not yet ready to answer.

Teach students the opening attention-getter:
**T:** *Come and sit close to me. It's time for...*
**S:** *CBeebies!*
Or
**T:** *1, 2, 3! It's time for...*
**S:** *CBeebies!*
Explain to students that whenever you use an attention-getter, they should stop talking and look at you.
Have students sit in a circle. Show students the visual schedule pictures. Ask for volunteers to help you turn them over. Encourage the whole class to say what each picture shows. Ask students to help you select the pictures that show today's schedule as you tell them what they are going to do today.

> **Note to teachers**
> You can also teach/review the attention-getter *All set? You bet!*

**Sing *Rainbow*.**

**Materials and preparation**
- Audio library – songs

Stick the cards around the room in the order of the song. Play *Rainbow* (track 17) and encourage students to sing along and dance.

## ACTIVE LEARNING

**Before watching the video – Look, it's a rainbow!**

**Materials and preparation**
- A picture of a rainbow
- Flashcards: *blue, green, orange, pink, purple, red, yellow*
- Two flyswatters (optional)

Sit together in a circle and show each flashcard slowly. Then show the picture of the rainbow. Divide the class into two groups and two lines facing the board. Stick the color flashcards on the board. Give the first student in each line a flyswatter. Call out a color and the first student in each group runs and swats the color you called out. These students then join the back of their line and the next two students listen, race, and swat. Continue until everyone has had a turn. If you don't have the flyswatters, students can touch the correct flashcard. You should set expectations of walking safely so as to avoid accidents.

> **Note to teachers**
> For big classes you can make three groups/lines to ensure students don't have to wait too long to have a turn. This is a recognition task so students don't need to say the word, but they can if you think they are ready.

**Watching the video – Let's watch!**

**Materials and preparation**
- Video library

Sit together so all students can see the screen/board. Play the video *Show Me Show Me, Series 1, Ep. 9, Music and rainbows* (video 7) and watch it together. Then play the video again and pause after each color is mentioned/shown in the video. Ask students what color it is and have them find and point to something in class with the same color (*blue, green,* or *red*).
You should set expectations of correct watching behavior, reminding students that they should sit still and watch quietly, respecting their classmates.

**After watching the video – Make a rainbow.**

**Materials and preparation**
- Audio library – songs
- Crepe paper: blue, green, orange, pink, purple, red, and yellow
- Glue
- Sheets of A4 poster paper

Ask students to go to their seats and give them a sheet of A4 poster paper. Put the crepe paper in the center of the table. Students take a piece of it at a time, tear a long strip, and stick it on the card to make a rainbow. Make the rainbow with the students, step by step. Monitor and help as needed.

> **Note to teachers**
> Play the *Rainbow song* (track 17) in the background and encourage students to sing along as they tear and stick.

## DIFFERENTIATED INSTRUCTION

**BELOW LEVEL**
**Before watching the video**
Pre-tear the strips of crepe paper and focus only on the colors from the video (blue, green, and red). Encourage students to recognize the three colors without overloading with all the colors.

**ABOVE LEVEL**
**Before watching the video**
Invite a student to call out a color for other students to find and swat/touch the flashcards. Then ask another student.

## CLOSING

**Sing *Rainbow*. Sing the *Goodbye song*.**

**Materials and preparation**
- Audio library – songs
- Sticky tape

Sing *Rainbow* (track 17) and encourage students to sing along. Pause the song and encourage them to keep singing without the music. Ask them to stick the finished rainbow craft on the classroom wall. Sing the *Goodbye song* (track 5) and invite students to sing along while they help you clean up the classroom. Encourage students to help each other. Say *goodbye* to them and have them say *goodbye* back to you.

**LOOK, COUNT, AND MATCH.**

CBEEBIES • WHAT IS A FAMILY? • UNIT 3  13

**Learning goals**
- Count from one to five
- Recognize numbers one to five
- Understand familiar words in a video

**Main language content**
Nature: *bee, butterfly, flower*
Numbers: *1-5*
Toys: *ball, car*
*How many (balls) can you see?*
*Let's count!*

# OPENING

**Circle time**

**Materials and preparation**
- A soft ball
- Puppet
- Visual schedule pictures

Say, *Hello, how are you?* to the puppet and encourage students to greet it with *hello* or *hi*. Have students sit in a circle. Roll the soft ball to a student and ask, *How are you?* Encourage them to answer (e.g. *I'm OK!*), roll the ball to a classmate, and ask them how they are. Repeat with other students as many times as possible.

> **Note to teachers**
> Encourage students to say how they are to as many classmates as possible to help create a learner-centered cooperative environment. Help them ask, *How are you?* by encouraging the class to ask in unison.

Remind students of the attention-getter and practice it with them:
**T:** *Come and sit close to me. It's time for…*
**S:** *CBeebies!*
Or
**T:** *1, 2, 3! It's time for…*
**S:** *CBeebies!*

> **Note to teachers**
> Remind students that they should be quiet and pay attention when you use the attention-getter.

Show them the visual schedule pictures. Choose a class helper of the day and have them order the pictures of the activities as they are mentioned.

**Sing *Five little monkeys*.**

**Materials and preparation**

- *Five little monkeys* song (easily found online; or any other song for numbers 1-5)

Stand together in a circle. Hold up one finger and say, *one*. Encourage students to copy you and continue up to number five. Repeat a few times, varying speed and volume. Play the *Five little monkeys* song (or any other song for numbers 1-5) and sing and dance together.

## ACTIVE LEARNING

### Before watching the video – Five balls

**Materials and preparation**

- A box
- Five balls
- Flashcards: *numbers 1-5*

Sit together in a circle and put the box with the five balls in the middle. Call out the number one and invite a student to get one ball out of the box, show to their classmates. Encourage them to say, *one*. Ask them to put the ball back in the box. Continue with numbers up to five. Slowly reveal the number flashcards and invite students to show you the number with their fingers.

> **Note to teachers**
> Don't insist on students producing at this stage. Having recognition tasks first will aid understanding and cementing language.

### Watching the video – Let's watch!

**Materials and preparation**

- Video library

Sit together and make sure all students can see the screen/board. Play the video *Num Tums, Series 1, Ep. 5* (video 8), and watch it together. Play it again and do the dance together at the start. Stop the video and count the hamsters and flowers together. Stop the video and have students stand in line, one behind the other, forming mini trains of five students. Have them count and move around the class. You should set expectations of walking safely so as to avoid accidents.
At the end, encourage students to air write the number five.
You should set expectations of correct watching behavior, reminding students that they should sit still and watch quietly, respecting their classmates.

### After watching the video – Look count, and match.

**Materials and preparation**

- Crayons
- Pencils
- Project Book page 13

Help students open their Project Books to page 13. Have students observe the page and ask, *How many (cars) can you see?* and count together. Encourage them to say, *one*, point to the number one on the page, and show how to draw a line between the number and the car. Repeat with the other numbers. Monitor and help as needed.

> **Note to teachers**
> Encourage students to count aloud as they match up the items. At the end, they can color the items and practice tracing the number with their fingers.

## DIFFERENTIATED INSTRUCTION

### BELOW LEVEL
**Before watching the video**
Introduce the numbers only for listening and counting using the box and balls. Allow students time to count together and take away the focus on number recognition.

### ABOVE LEVEL
**Before watching the video**
Stick the number flashcards randomly around the room. Students stand together in the center of the room: call out a number randomly and students look, find, and run to the number.

## CLOSING

### Look and count. Sing the *Goodbye song*.

**Materials and preparation**

- Audio library – songs
- Flashcards: *numbers 1-5*

Stick the flashcards on the board. Stand together in a circle, count from 1 to 5 on your fingers together, and ask students to point to the correct flashcard. Monitor and help as needed.
Sing the *Goodbye song* (track 5) and invite students to sing along while they clean up and put their things away. Encourage students to help each other. Show each number flashcard while they say *goodbye* to the numbers.

# OPENING

## Circle time

**Materials and preparation**
- A soft ball
- Audio library – songs
- Puppet
- Visual schedule pictures

Stand together in a circle and sing the *Hello song* (track 4). Give students the soft ball to pass on to other students and say, *hello*. Say, *Hello, how are you?* to the puppet and encourage students to greet it with *hello* or *hi*.

> **Note to teachers**
> Encourage students to greet as many classmates as possible to help create a learner-centered, cooperative environment.

Remind students of the attention-getter and practice it with them:
**T:** *Come and sit close to me. It's time for...*
**S:** *CBeebies!*
Or
**T:** *1, 2, 3! It's time for...*
**S:** *CBeebies!*

> **Note to teachers**
> You can also teach/review the attention-getter *All set? You bet!*

Have students sit in a circle. Show each visual schedule picture and then separate the ones that show the activities of today's class. Have a volunteer place the activities in the center of the circle.

**Learning goals**
- Count to five
- Develop cognitive and motor skills
- Use visuals to understand a video

**Main language content**
Nature: *flowers, petals*
Numbers: *1-5*
*How many (flowers) can you see?*
*Let's count!*

**Sing Five little monkeys.**

**Materials and preparation**

- *Five little monkeys* song (easily found online; or any other song for numbers 1-5)

Stand together in a circle. Hold up one finger and say, *one*. Encourage students to copy you and continue up to number five. Repeat but in reverse (counting down from 5 to 1). Play the *Five little monkeys* song (or any other song for numbers 1-5) and sing and dance together.

# ACTIVE LEARNING

**Before watching the video – Five-petal flower**

**Materials and preparation**

- A flower with five petals (artificial or craft)
- Flashcards: *numbers 1-5*

Sit together in a circle and show each of the flashcards counting together with the students. Put the numbers down in a line. Show students the flower and together count the petals.

> **Note to teachers**
> Encourage students to count with less help from you. Point to the first petal and say, *one*. Then point to the second petal and have them say, *two*.

**Watching the video – Let's watch!**

**Materials and preparation**

- Video library

Sit together and make sure all students can see the screen/board. Play the video *Num Tums, Series 1, Ep. 5* (video 8), and watch it together. Play the video again and encourage students to count aloud together. Play it a third time and as you watch, call out a number and invite students to point to the screen when this number is shown. They can also say, *There it is!* You should set expectations of correct watching behavior, reminding students that they should sit still and watch quietly, respecting their classmates.

**After watching video – Make a five-petal flower.**

**Materials and preparation**

- Play dough (different colors)
- Popsicle sticks
- Sheets of paper (one per student; optional)

Give some play dough to students. Show them how to make a ball and flat it. Have them do it five times to create five "petals." Students join the petals to make a flower. They can use the popsicle stick to make the flower stalk. Encourage them to count to five.

> **Note to teachers**
> Students can stick the play dough creating their flower in a sheet of paper. If possible, take pictures of students' work.

# DIFFERENTIATED INSTRUCTION

## BELOW LEVEL
**Before watching the video**

Put the number flashcards in a long line down the center of the room. In pairs, students go along the line and say the numbers in sequence. Help them to say each number.

## ABOVE LEVEL
**Before watching the video**

**Materials and preparation**

- Small cards with numbers 1-5 written on each card (one card per student)

Give each student a card. Call out a number; students with that number hold up their card. Have them switch cards several times, and call out different numbers.

# CLOSING

**Sing *Five little monkeys*. Sing the Goodbye song.**

**Materials and preparation**

- Audio library – songs
- *Five little monkeys* song (easily found online; or any other song for numbers 1-5)

Stand together in a circle. Hold up one finger and say, *one*. Play the *Five little monkeys* song (or any other song for numbers 1-5) and encourage students to sing and move along while they clean up and put their things away. Encourage students to help each other. Play the *Goodbye song* (track 5). Say *goodbye* to them and have them say *goodbye* back to you.

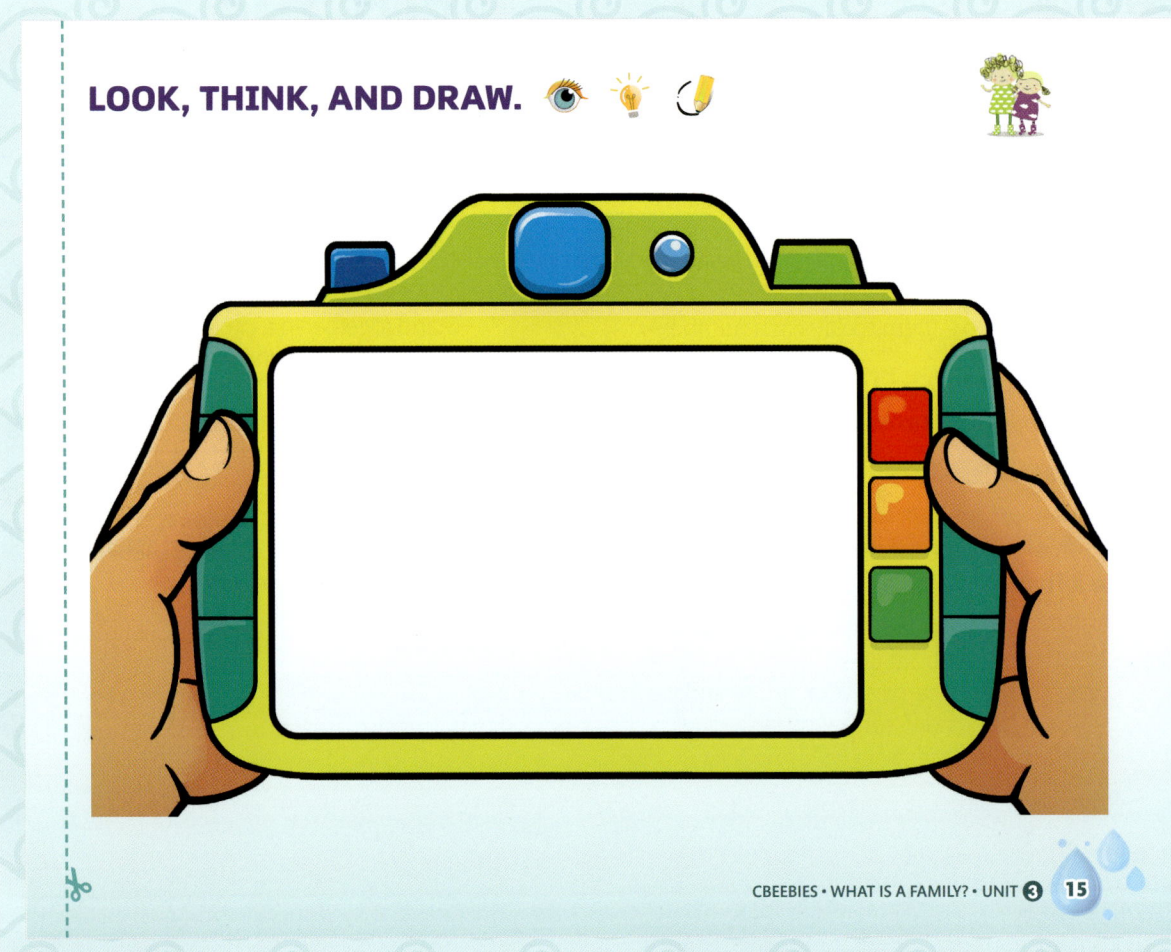

**Learning goals**
- Develop fine motor skills in context
- Practice words for family members
- Understand familiar words in a video

**Main language content**
Family: *baby, dad, mom*
*It's a family picture. That's (my mom). Let's take a picture.*

# OPENING

**Circle time**

**Materials and preparation**
- Visual schedule pictures (hide them around the classroom)

Say, *Hello, how are you?* to the puppet and encourage students to greet it with *hello* or *hi*. Ask, *How are you?* Encourage them to answer (e.g. *I'm OK!*) and ask a classmate how they are.

Remind students of the attention-getter and practice it with them:
**T:** *Come and sit close to me. It's time for…*
**S:** *CBeebies!*
Or
**T:** *1, 2, 3! It's time for…*
**S:** *CBeebies!*

> **Note to teachers**
> Remind students that they should be quiet and pay attention when you use the attention-getter.

Hide the visual schedule pictures that refer to today's activities. Tell students to look for them around the classroom. As they find a picture, tell them to hand it to you. Then talk to students about each of the moments of the class.

**Play *Musical statues*.**

**Materials and preparation**
- Audio library – songs (or another song students like)

Play a song from the audio library or any other song students like. Invite students to move/walk around the classroom to the music. When you stop the music, students have to freeze in whatever position they are in and they can't wobble. You should set expectations of walking safely as to avoid accidents.

> **Note to teachers**
> This activity is to give the idea of a picture being a moment frozen in time.

# ACTIVE LEARNING

## Before watching the video – Family pictures

### Materials and preparation
- Pictures of families (different types of family and from different ethnic groups; at least one with a baby)

Sit together in a circle. Show students one of the pictures and ask students who they can see. Introduce/review the words for family members, focusing on *mom*, *dad*, and *baby*. Stick the other pictures up around the classroom and, together, walk to each picture and talk about what you can see. Invite groups of students to act out posing for a family picture and others, taking a picture.

> **Note to teachers**
> Use pictures of different family types and people in order to be as inclusive as possible.

## Watching the video – Let's watch!

### Materials and preparation
- Video library

Sit together and make sure all students can see the screen/board. Play the video *Nelly and Nora, Ep. 19, Family Photos* (video 9), and watch it together. Pause to ask students who is in the family pictures Nelly and Nora are looking at. At the end, ask why they are taking pictures of and what the weather is like.

You should set expectations of correct watching behavior, reminding students that they should sit still and watch quietly, respecting their classmates.

## After watching the video – Look, think, and draw.

### Materials and preparation
- Colored pencils and crayons
- Project Book page 15

Help students open their Project Books to page 15. Ask them, *What's it?* and listen to their answers. Say, *It's a camera!* and have them repeat after you. Tell students they are going to draw a family in the camera view. Encourage students to include details, such as the weather.

> **Note to teachers**
> Students can choose to draw their family or any family picture they like.

# DIFFERENTIATED INSTRUCTION

## BELOW LEVEL
### Before watching the video
Focus on describing just one family picture that include *mom*, *dad*, and *baby*. Extend by inviting students to act out the pictures.

## ABOVE LEVEL
### After watching the video
Once students have finished drawing their family, put students into pairs or small groups and invite them to share and compare their drawings.

# CLOSING

## Sing *Clean up time*. Sing the *Goodbye song*.

### Materials and preparation
- Audio library – songs

Clean up together and sing *Clean up time* (track 11). Encourage students to help each other put their things away. Sing the *Goodbye song* (track 5) and invite students to sing along. Say *goodbye* to them and have them say *goodbye* back to you.

# Unit 4 Do you share your toys?

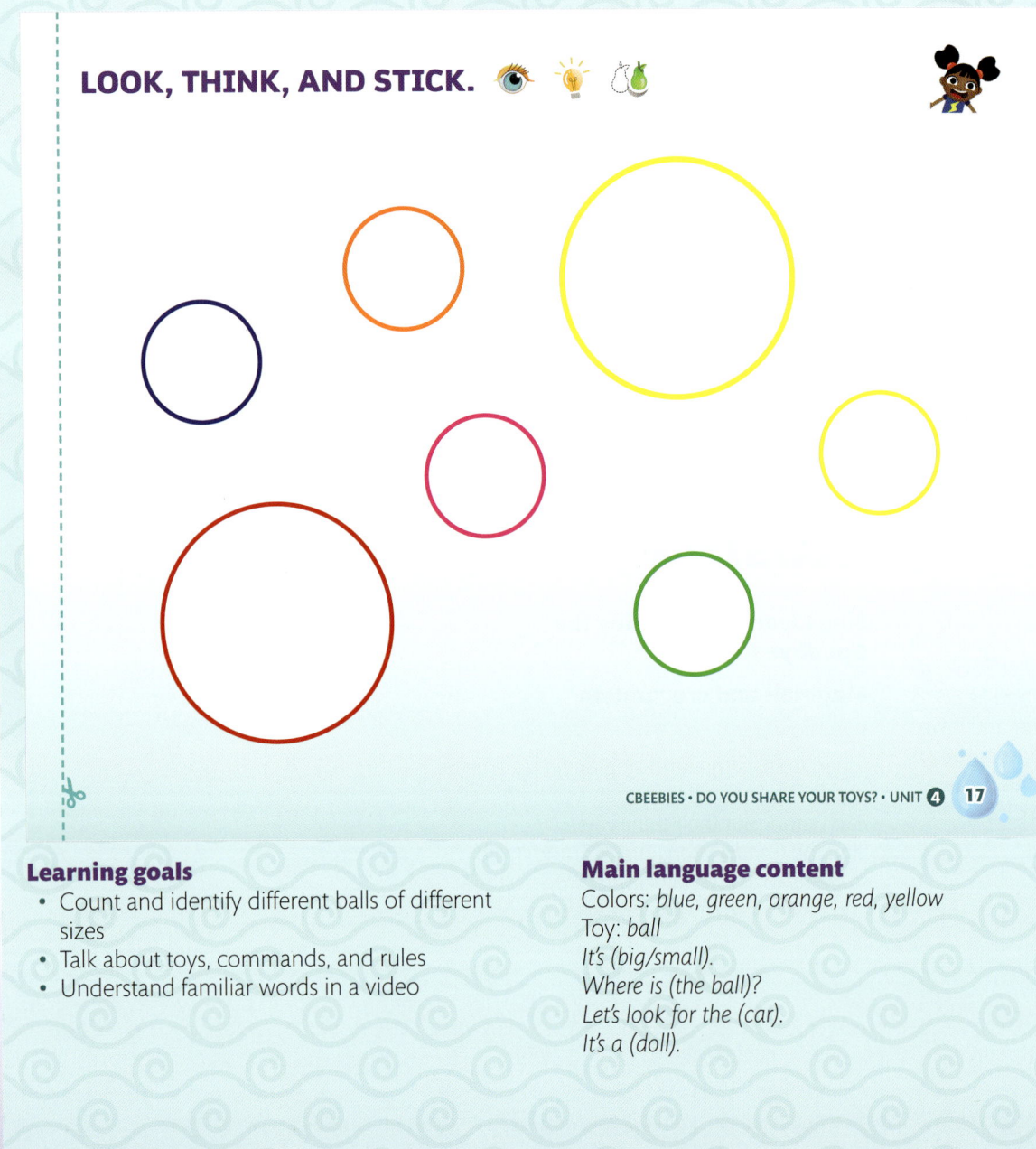

## Learning goals
- Count and identify different balls of different sizes
- Talk about toys, commands, and rules
- Understand familiar words in a video

## Main language content
Colors: *blue, green, orange, red, yellow*
Toy: *ball*
*It's (big/small).*
*Where is (the ball)?*
*Let's look for the (car).*
*It's a (doll).*

## OPENING

### Circle time

**Materials and preparation**
- A soft ball
- Audio library – songs
- Puppet
- Visual schedule pictures

Stand together in a circle and sing the *Hello song* (track 4). Give students the soft ball to pass on to other students and say, *hello*. Say, *Hello, how are you?* to the puppet and encourage students to do the same.

> **Note to teachers**
> If students are confident about this Circle time routine, you can say what the weather looks like today and encourage them to repeat after you, e.g. *Today it's (sunny).*

Remind students of the attention-getter and practice it with them:
**T:** *Come and sit close to me. It's time for…*
**S:** *CBeebies!*
Or
**T:** *1, 2, 3! It's time for…*
**S:** *CBeebies!*

Explain to students that whenever you use an attention-getter, they should stop talking and look at you.
Have students sit in a circle. Show students the visual schedule pictures. Ask for volunteers to help you turn them over. Encourage the whole class to say what each picture shows. Ask students to help you select the pictures that show today's schedule as you tell them what they are going to do today.

> **Note to teachers**
> You can also teach/review the attention-getter *All set? You bet!*

### Colored balls search

**Materials and preparation**

- Five balls (blue, green, orange, red, and yellow; one of each)

Hide the balls around the classroom. Ask, *Where is the green ball?* Say, *Let's look for the green ball*. Together, go around the room looking for the green ball. Repeat with the other balls. You should set expectations of walking safely so as to avoid accidents.

## ACTIVE LEARNING

### Before watching the video – What color is the ball?

**Materials and preparation**

- A box
- Five balls (blue, green, orange, red, and yellow; one of each)

Put the balls in the box. Sit together in a circle, put the box with the balls in the center of the circle. Pull out a ball and say the color (e.g. *blue*) to model the activity for students. Put the ball back into the box and invite each student at a time to take a ball out and say the color. Monitor and help as needed. Encourage the students to help each other saying the correct color.

> **Note to teachers**
> If you think it is appropriate, you can encourage students to say, *It's a (blue) ball*. At the end and if you have time, a volunteer student can ask a classmate to find and take out a particular ball from the box.

### Watching the video – Let's watch!

**Materials and preparation**

- Video library

Sit together and make sure all students can see the screen/board. Play the video *Yakka Dee, Ep. 16, Ball* (video 10), and watch it together. Play the video again and pause it at each different colored ball in the video, and have students say the color.
You should set expectations of correct watching behavior, reminding students that they should sit still and watch quietly, respecting their classmates.

### After watching the video – Look, think, and stick.

**Materials and preparation**

- Project Book page 17

Help students open their Project Books to page 17. Point to the different circles on page and ask students to say each color. Help them turn to the stickers page at the back of the book and identify the ball stickers, focusing on size and color. Help them peel off the sticker and stick it on the correct circle on page 17. Monitor and help as needed.

> **Note to teachers**
> At the end, encourage students to point to each ball, and say its color and size.

## DIFFERENTIATED INSTRUCTION

### BELOW LEVEL
**After watching the video**

Work together sticking only one sticker at a time. Invite students to only find the blue ball and then stick that before moving on to the next sticker.

### ABOVE LEVEL
**After watching the video**

Point to the blue ball and say, *I like blue balls. What about you?* Encourage students to point to a colored ball they like and repeat the sentence changing the color name when necessary.

## CLOSING

### Say the color. Sing the *Goodbye song*.

**Materials and preparation**

- Audio library – songs
- Five balls (blue, green, orange, red, and yellow; one of each)

Have students sit in a circle and put all the balls in the center of the circle. Roll a ball to a student and have them say the color. Have them roll the ball to another classmate repeating the color. Repeat with another ball and roll it to another student. Alternatively, you can say the corresponding color (sometimes you say the correct color, and other times, you say the wrong color) and have students say, *yes* or *no*.

Sing the *Goodbye song* (track 5) and invite students to sing along while they put their things away. Encourage students to help each other. Say *goodbye* to them and have them say *goodbye* back to you.

**Learning goals**
- Develop creative and imaginative skills
- Talk about toys, commands, and rules
- Understand familiar words in a video

**Main language content**
Toys: *ball, bike, doll, teddy*
*I like my (blue) (bike).*
*It's a funny ball.*

# OPENING

**Circle time**

**Materials and preparation**
- A soft ball
- Puppet
- Visual schedule pictures

Say, *Hello, how are you?* to the puppet and encourage students to greet it with *hello* or *hi*. Have students sit in a circle. Roll the soft ball to a student and ask, *How are you?* Encourage them to answer (e.g. *I'm OK!*), roll the ball to a classmate, and ask them how they are. Repeat with other students as many times as possible.

> **Note to teachers**
> If you think it is appropriate, divide students into groups of five. They sit together asking and answering, *How are you?*

Remind students of the attention-getter and practice it with them:
**T:** *Come and sit close to me. It's time for…*
**S:** *CBeebies!*
Or
**T:** *1, 2, 3! It's time for…*
**S:** *CBeebies!*

> **Note to teachers**
> Remind students that they should be quiet and pay attention when you use the attention-getter.

Show them the visual schedule pictures. Choose a class helper of the day and have them order the pictures of the activities as they are mentioned.

**My toys**

**Materials and preparation**
- A sheet of paper
- Flashcards: *ball, bike, doll, teddy*

Sit together in a circle and use the sheet of paper to cover the flashcards. Reveal each flashcard by slowly lifting the sheet off the paper and have students guess what it is before revealing it completely. Say, *I like my (bike)*. Stick the flashcards on the wall around the classroom. Stand together in the middle and call out a toy. Students listen, look, and run to the correct toy. Encourage them to say, *I like my (bike)* each time they run to a flashcard. You should set expectations of walking safely so as to avoid accidents.

## ACTIVE LEARNING

**Before watching the video – Pick the ball.**

**Materials and preparation**
- A box
- Several colored balls (blue, green, orange, red, and yellow)

Put the balls into the box. Pick out a ball and say, *It's a (blue) ball, I like my (blue) ball*. Invite students to come, pick a ball, and say the color. Monitor and help as needed. Put all the balls out and call out a sequence of balls, e.g. *blue ball, yellow ball, red ball*. Ask a volunteer student to put the balls in the correct sequence. Repeat a few times with different students.

> **Note to teachers**
> Students are not expected to say the full sentence (e.g. *I like my blue ball*) at this stage. A thumbs up is fine and shows some understanding.

**Watching the video – Let's watch!**

**Materials and preparation**
- Video library

Sit together and make sure all students can see the screen/board. Play the video *Yakka Dee, Ep. 16, Ball* (video 10), and watch it together. Say the colors as you see them and encourage students to do repeat. Stop at the "funny" ball and focus on the meaning of *funny*. Practice saying, *ball* and air draw a circle shape together.
You should set expectations of correct watching behavior, reminding students that they should sit still and watch quietly, respecting their classmates.

**After watching the video – Make a funny ball.**

**Materials and preparation**
- Poster paper cut into a circle (one per student)
- Colored pencils and crayons
- Crepe paper
- Glitter
- Glue
- Popsicle stick (optional)

Give each student a poster paper circle and some art supplies (glitter, glue, crepe paper, colored pencils, and crayons). Tell students they are going to make a "funny ball." Students stick glitter and crepe paper to decorate their balls.

> **Note to teachers**
> Encourage students to be as creative as they want. At the end, glue a popsicle stick to each paper circle and students can hold up their "funny balls."

## DIFFERENTIATED INSTRUCTION

### BELOW LEVEL
**Before watching the video**
Focus only on the color names recognition. Call out a color and ask students to take the corresponding ball from the box.

### ABOVE LEVEL
**Before watching the video**
A student can call out a color, and a classmate goes and takes the corresponding ball, saying its color or the full sentence, *It's a (blue) ball* or simply *It's (blue)*.

## CLOSING

**Play with balls. Sing the *Goodbye song*.**

**Materials and preparation**
- Audio library – songs
- Balls (per pair or trios of students)
- Students' ball crafts

Have students sit in a circle and ask them to show their balls. Invite them to play with their balls. Introduce the idea of 2D/3D shapes by asking them to try to roll their balls, and then roll a real ball to see the difference. You don't need to introduce any new language here, simply familiarize students with the concept. Sing the *Goodbye song* (track 5). Say *goodbye* to them and have them say *goodbye* back to you.

**Learning goals**
- Count to five
- Recognize numbers and develop motor skills
- Watch and follow a story in a video

**Main language content**
Nature: *moon, stars*
Numbers: *1-5*
Toy: *ball*
*It's round.*
*How many stars can you see?*
*Let's count!*
*Look! There are five stars.*

# OPENING

**Circle time**

**Materials and preparation**
- A soft ball
- Audio library – songs
- Puppet
- Visual schedule pictures

Stand together in a circle and sing the *Hello song* (track 4). Give students the soft ball to pass on to other students and say, *hello*. Say, *Hello, how are you?* to the puppet and encourage students to greet it with *hello* or *hi*.

> **Note to teachers**
> If students are confident about this Circle time routine, you can say what the weather is like today and encourage them to repeat after you, e.g. *Today it's (sunny)*.

Remind students of the attention-getter and practice it with them:
**T:** *Come and sit close to me. It's time for...*
**S:** *CBeebies!*
Or
**T:** *1, 2, 3! It's time for...*
**S:** *CBeebies!*

> **Note to teachers**
> You can also teach/review the attention-getter *All set? You bet!*

Have students sit in a circle. Show each visual schedule picture and then separate the ones that show the activities of today's class. Have a volunteer place the activities in the center of the circle.

**Sing the *Clap* song.**

**Materials and preparation**

- Audio library - songs

Sit together in a circle and sing the *Clap* song (track 9). Encourage students to join in with singing and clapping. If students are familiar with the rhythm, continue the song and sing up to five.

# ACTIVE LEARNING

**Before watching the video – Look at the moon and the stars.**

**Materials and preparation**

- Pictures of the moon and five stars (cutouts)

Have students sit in a circle and show the picture of the *moon* cutout. Say, *Look at the moon! It's round* and circle it with your finger. Show students the stars one by one and count as you show them. Put the picture of the *moon* in the center of the circle. Invite students to put the stars around the moon. Have them count as they place the pictures of the stars.

> **Note to teachers**
>
> You can also play *Who wants to be the moon?* Select one student to be the moon and the other students are stars around the moon. Play a song that students like and have them say, *moon* or *star*.

**Watching the video – Let's watch!**

**Materials and preparation**

- Video library

Sit together and make sure everyone can see the screen/board. Play the video *Num Tums, Series 1, Ep. 15, More number 5* (video 11), and watch it together. Play it again, pause and count the items together. Ask students to point out to number 5. You should set expectations of correct watching behavior, reminding students that they should sit still and watch quietly, respecting their classmates.

**After watching the video – Draw the moon and five stars.**

**Materials and preparation**

- Colored pencils or crayons
- Crepe paper (yellow)
- Glitter (optional)
- Glue
- Large circle rulers or other large circle-shaped object to be used as a ruler (one per four students; optional)
- Sheets of paper (one per student)

Give each student a sheet of paper and tell them to draw a moon in the center of the page. If students struggle with drawing it, help them use a ruler to do so. Give each student some yellow crepe paper. Tell students there is one star next to the moon and show students how to tear a piece of the yellow crepe paper and stick it next to the moon. Repeat and continue up to number 5.

> **Note to teachers**
>
> If possible, use glitter to decorate the moon surface and the stars.

# DIFFERENTIATED INSTRUCTION

**BELOW LEVEL**
**Before watching the video**

Stick the moon and the stars pictures in sequence on the board and count each one together.

**ABOVE LEVEL**
**Before watching the video**

**Materials and preparation**

- Number cards: *1-5* (one card per student)

Give the cards to the students. Put some stars (e.g. three stars) in the center of the circle and have students hold up the corresponding number card. Repeat with other numbers of stars.

# CLOSING

**Say goodbye to the moon and stars. Sing the *Goodbye song*.**

**Materials and preparation**

- Audio library – songs
- Student's moon and stars crafts

Invite students to stand together with the moon and stars craft. Encourage them to say, *Goodbye, moon; goodbye, stars.* Count the stars again.
Sing the *Goodbye song* (track 5) and invite students to sing along while they help you clean up the classroom. Encourage students to help each other. Say *goodbye* to them and have them say *goodbye* back to you.

**Learning goals**
- Develop cognitive and motor skills in context
- Talk about toys, commands, and rules
- Understand an animated video

**Main language content**
Toys: *ball, scooter, teddy, tractor, trumpet*
*I like (balls).*
*My favorite toy is the (ball).*

# OPENING

**Materials and preparation**
- Puppet
- Visual schedule pictures (hide them around the classroom)

Say, *Hello, how are you?* to the puppet and encourage students to greet it with *hello* or *hi*. Ask, *How are you?* Encourage them to answer (e.g. *I'm OK!*) and ask a classmate how they are.

Remind students of the attention-getter and practice it with them:
**T:** *Come and sit close to me. It's time for…*
**S:** *CBeebies!*
Or
**T:** *1, 2, 3! It's time for…*
**S:** *CBeebies!*

> **Note to teachers**
> Remind students that they should be quiet and pay attention when you use the attention-getter.

Hide the visual schedule pictures that refer to today's activities. Tell students to look for them around the classroom. As they find a picture, tell them to hand it to you. Then talk to students about each of the moments of the class.

**Find the toys!**

**Materials and preparation**
- Pictures of ball, scooter, teddy, tractor, and trumpet (or real toys, if possible)

Hide the pictures around the classroom. Tell students they have to find the pictures of the toys. Students walk around to find the pictures (or real toys) and bring them to the front of the class. Say the name of each toy and have them repeat after you. Mix them up, call out a toy, and have students find it.

## ACTIVE LEARNING

### Before watching the video – What's missing?

**Materials and preparation**
- A large sheet of paper (to cover the pictures)
- Pictures of a ball, scooter, teddy, tractor, and trumpet

Sit together in a circle. Spread the pictures in a line in the center of the circle. Cover the pictures using the sheet of paper. Remove a picture, without students seeing it. Ask them what toy is missing.

> **Note to teachers**
> Encourage students to tell you which of the toys they like best.

### Watching the video – Let's watch!

**Materials and preparation**
- Video library

Sit together and make sure everyone can see the screen. Play the video *Nelly and Nora, Ep. 27, Cooking up a Storm* (video 12), and watch it together. Pause to say the toys you can see. Mime using the toys and say the words.
Ask students what the weather is like and focus on the clouds.
You should set expectations of correct watching behavior, reminding students that they should sit still and watch quietly, respecting their classmates.

### After watching the video – Look, think, and draw.

**Materials and preparation**
- Crayons
- Pencils
- Project book page 19

Help students open their Project Books to page 19. Ask them what toys they can see. Show students how to trace the other half of the toys to complete the pictures.

> **Note to teachers**
> Fast finishers can color the toys.

## DIFFERENTIATED INSTRUCTION

### BELOW LEVEL
**Before watching the video**

Focus on recognition, rather than production. You can ask students, *What's missing? The car?* And have students answer *yes* or *no*.

### ABOVE LEVEL
**After watching the video**

**Materials and preparation**
- Sheets of paper

Students can draw their favorite toy.

## CLOSING

### Talk about toys. Sing the *Goodbye song*.

**Materials and preparation**
- Audio library – songs

Ask students about their favorite toys. Allow them to use L1 as needed.
Sing the *Goodbye song* (track 5) and invite students to sing along as they help you clean up the classroom. Say *goodbye* to them and have them say *goodbye* back to you.

# Unit 5 How do you help at home?

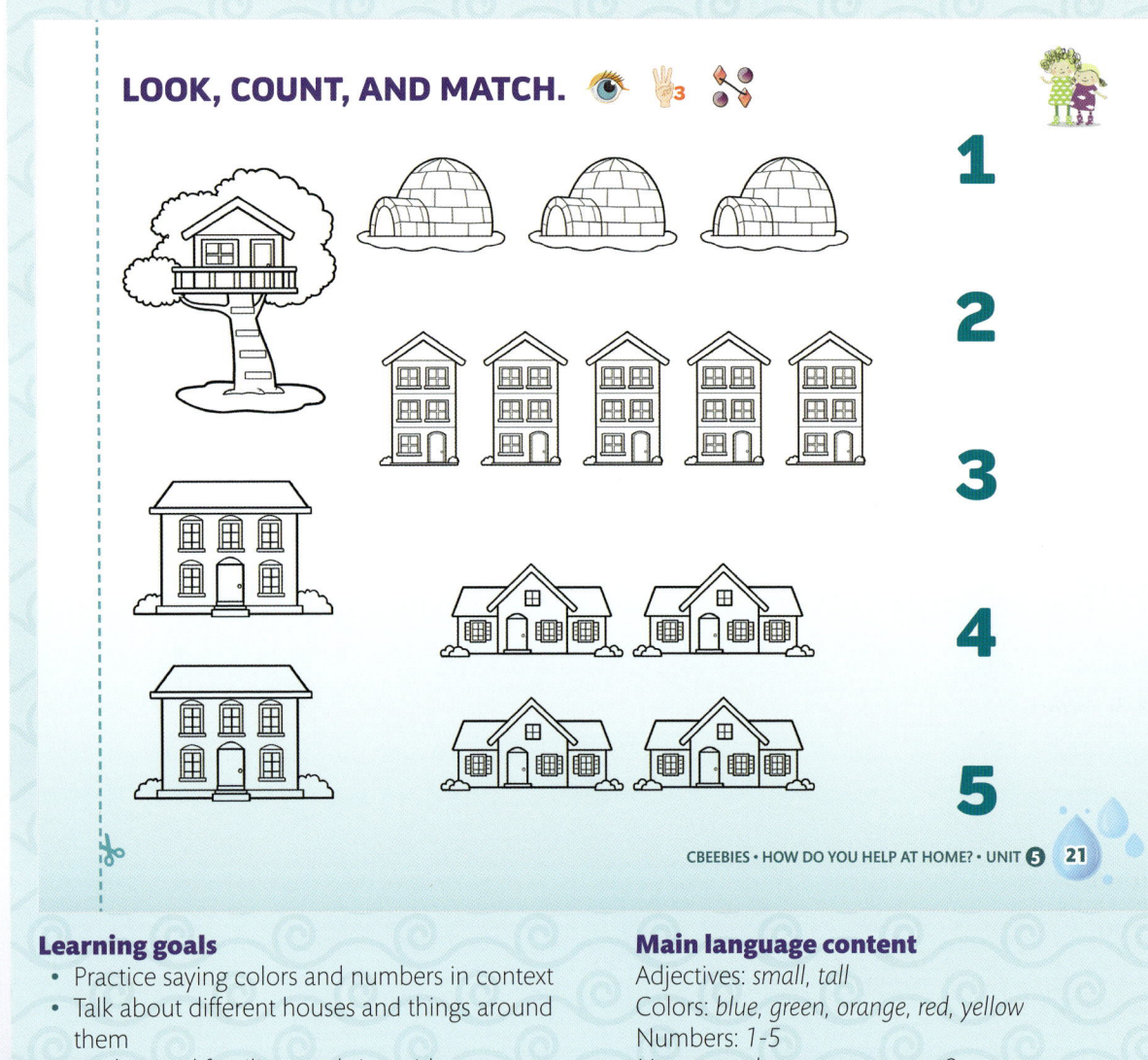

**Learning goals**
- Practice saying colors and numbers in context
- Talk about different houses and things around them
- Understand familiar words in a video

**Main language content**
Adjectives: *small, tall*
Colors: *blue, green, orange, red, yellow*
Numbers: *1-5*
*How many houses can you see?*
*What color is/are the house(s)?*

## OPENING

**Circle time**

**Materials and preparation**
- A soft ball
- Audio library – songs
- Puppet
- Visual schedule pictures

Stand together in a circle and sing the *Hello song* (track 4). Give students the soft ball to pass on to other students and say, *hello*. Say, *Hello, how are you?* to the puppet and encourage students to do the same. Ask students what the weather is like today. Mime *sunny*, *cloudy*, and *rainy* together.

> **Note to teachers**
> If you have a weather chart and cards available, you can invite a volunteer students to stick up the card for the weather.

Remind students of the attention-getter and practice it with them:
**T:** *Come and sit close to me. It's time for…*
**S:** *CBeebies!*
Or
**T:** *1, 2, 3! It's time for…*
**S:** *CBeebies!*
Explain to students that whenever you use an attention-getter, they should stop talking and look at you.
Have students sit in a circle. Show students the visual schedule pictures. Ask for volunteers to help you turn them over. Encourage the whole class to say what each picture shows. Ask students to help you select the pictures that show today's schedule as you tell them what they are going to do today.

> **Note to teachers**
> You can also teach/review the attention-getter *All set? You bet!*

**Sing, move, and dance.**

**Materials and preparation**
- Audio library – songs

Stand together in a circle and sing any song students like; have them sing along and join in with the actions. Encourage everyone to participate.

# ACTIVE LEARNING

**Before watching the video – Houses all around**

**Materials and preparation**
- Pictures of a red house, two green houses, three yellow houses, four blue houses, five orange houses, a tall house, a small house
- Two flyswatters (optional)

Sit together in a circle and slowly reveal the picture of a *small house* and a *tall house*. Say, *small* and *tall* as you them the pictures. Show students the picture of the red house and ask what color it is and how many houses they can see (*one*). Repeat with the other pictures of houses.
Stick all the house pictures on the board. Divide the class into two groups and give the first student in each group a flyswatter (if available). Call out *three yellow houses*. Have students look, find, walk, and swater (or touch) the correct picture(s). Continue with the next student in the line.

> **Note to teachers**
> With big classes divide the class into three groups to maximize student involvement. Encourage students who are waiting in line to chant the words.

**Watching the video – Let's watch!**

**Materials and preparation**
- Video library

Sit together and make sure all students can see the screen/board. Play the video *Yakka Dee, Ep. 13, House* (video 13), and watch it together. Play the video again and pause it at *small house* and *tall house*; encourage students to say the words *small* and *tall* and make the corresponding gestures. Continue playing the video and pause again at the colored houses. Encourage students to say the colors and count them together.
You should set expectations of correct watching behavior, reminding students that they should sit still and watch quietly, respecting their classmates.

**After watching the video – Look, count, and match.**

**Materials and preparation**
- Crayons
- Pencils
- Project Book page 21

Help students open their Project Books to page 21. Count the houses together. Students trace the outline of each house with a pencil and count as they trace. You can tell them what colors to use to color the houses or they can choose.

> **Note to teachers**
> To practice number formation, air write the numbers together.

# DIFFERENTIATED INSTRUCTION

**BELOW LEVEL**
**Before watching the video**
Instead of asking students to put together the full phrase, encourage students to say either the number or the color only.

**ABOVE LEVEL**
**After watching the video**
After students have finished, ask them about their houses. Encourage students to tell you the number of the houses and the color, e.g. *three pink houses*.

# CLOSING

**An igloo or a treehouse? Sing the *Goodbye song*.**

**Materials and preparation**
- Audio library – songs

Sit with students in a circle. Ask students to look at the pictures of houses in their Project Books, and encourage them to describe them. Point to the treehouse and igloo. Ask, *Who lives here? Which one do you prefer?* Encourage students to share whether they would prefer to live in a tree house or an igloo and to give their reasons. Play the *Goodbye song* (track 5). Say *goodbye* to them and have them say *goodbye* back to you.

**Learning goals**
- Talk about different houses and places in the house
- Understand what a lighthouse is
- Explain understanding of a video

**Main language content**
Places and elements: *boat, light, lighthouse, rock*
*Shine your light!*
*Danger, danger!*
*Sail, sail around the rocks.*

# OPENING

## Circle time

### Materials and preparation
- A soft ball
- Puppet
- Visual schedule pictures

Say, *Hello, how are you?* to the puppet and encourage students to greet it with *hello* or *hi*. Have students sit in a circle. Roll the soft ball to a student and ask, *How are you?* Encourage them to answer (e.g. *I'm OK!*), roll the ball to a classmate and ask them how they are. Repeat with other students as many times as possible. Ask students what the weather is like today. Mime *sunny, cloudy,* and *rainy* together.

> **Note to teachers**
> If you have a weather chart and cards available, you can invite a volunteer student to stick up the card for the weather.

Remind students of the attention-getter and practice it with them:
**T:** *Come and sit close to me. It's time for…*
**S:** *CBeebies!*
Or
**T:** *1, 2, 3! It's time for…*
**S:** *CBeebies!*

> **Note to teachers**
> Remind students that they should be quiet and pay attention when you use the attention-getter.

Show them the visual schedule pictures. Choose a class helper of the day and have them order the pictures of the activities as they are mentioned.

**Play *Musical chairs*.**

**Materials and preparation**

- Audio library – songs

Arrange the classroom chairs (matching the number of students) in a big circle facing outward. Play some music and students move around the chairs. Stop the music and everyone sits down. Take away a chair and play again. Stop the music again and ask students to race to sit on a chair. There is one seat messing. The student who is standing says a color or a number. Continue playing as many times as possible.

# ACTIVE LEARNING

**Before watching the video – Point and say.**

**Materials and preparation**

- Pictures of a lighthouse, boat, and rock

Show students the picture of a lighthouse printout. Make gestures acting out a lighthouse and shine your light all around. Invite students join you with the movements and gestures.
Show students the pictures of the rock and boat flashcards. Mime being a big rock, standing still, and rowing a boat. Stick the pictures on the board, point to a picture, and students mime being the object.

> **Note to teachers**
> Ask students if they know what a lighthouse is, if they've ever seen one, and what they think they are for.

**Watching the video – Let's watch!**

**Materials and preparation**

- Video library

Sit together and make sure everyone can see the screen/board. Play *Show Me Show Me, Series 6, Ep. 9, Gardening and lighthouses* (video 14), and watch it together. Play it again and pause at the lighthouse, rock, and boat. Invite students to mime being these objects and try to say the words. Ask students about the lighthouse, encouraging them to use the words *tall* and *small*, and say the colors. You should set expectations of correct watching behavior, reminding students that they should sit still and watch quietly, respecting their classmates.

**After watching the video – Be a lighthouse.**

Divide the class into three groups. One group are lighthouses, the other group are rocks and the final group are boats. Everyone acts out their part and the boats safely sail around the rocks. Switch groups around so every group gets to be the lighthouse, the rock and the boat at least once.

> **Note to teachers**
> With big classes set up two sets of groups and have them work simultaneously at each end of the classroom.

# DIFFERENTIATED INSTRUCTION

**BELOW LEVEL**
**Before watching the video**
Focus only on the lighthouse picture and mime being a lighthouse together.

**ABOVE LEVEL**
**After watching the video**
Get the lighthouse group to say, *Shine my light*; the rocks group to say, *Danger, danger!*; and the boat group to say, *Sail, sail around the rocks*.

# CLOSING

**Play *The boat's rocking*. Sing the *Goodbye song*.**

**Materials and preparation**

- Audio library – songs

Ask students to sit on the floor in pairs, one pair behind the other. Tell them to pretend to row a boat. Every so often, call out, *Oh, no! The boat is rocking*. Students mime rocking in their boats.
Sing the *Goodbye song* (track 5) and have students sing along. Say *goodbye* to them and have them say *goodbye* back to you.

**Learning goals**
- Identify what is in the kitchen
- Talk about different houses and places in the house
- Understand familiar words in a video

**Main language content**
In the house: *kitchen*
In the kitchen: *cabinets, faucet, freezer, refrigerator sink, stove*

# OPENING

## Circle time

**Materials and preparation**
- A soft ball
- Audio library – songs
- Puppet
- Visual schedule pictures

Stand together in a circle and sing the *Hello song* (track 4). Give students the soft ball to pass on to other students and say, *hello*. Say, *Hello, how are you?* to the puppet and encourage students to greet it with *hello* or *hi*. Ask students what the weather is like today. Mime *sunny*, *cloudy*, and *rainy* together.

> **Note to teachers**
> If you have a weather chart and cards available, you can invite a volunteer student to stick up the card for the weather.

Remind students of the attention-getter and practice it with them:
**T:** *Come and sit close to me. It's time for…*
**S:** *CBeebies!*
Or
**T:** *1, 2, 3! It's time for…*
**S:** *CBeebies!*

> **Note to teachers**
> You can also teach/review the attention-getter *All set? You bet!*

Have students sit in a circle. Show each visual schedule picture and then separate the ones that show the activities of today's class. Have a volunteer place the activities in the center of the circle.

## Let's explore the kitchen.

### Materials and preparation
- A large picture of a kitchen (showing cabinets, faucet, freezer, refrigerator, sink, stove)

Sit together in a circle. Show students the picture of the kitchen. Ask students what they can see. Together, mime being at the sink and turning on the faucet, washing the dishes. Mime opening the fridge and looking inside. Mime opening cabinets and taking out plates and cups. Mime cooking some food at the stove.

# ACTIVE LEARNING

### Before watching the video – What's this?

### Materials and preparation
- Pictures of cabinets, faucet, freezer, refrigerator, sink, stove
- Two flyswatters (optional)

Sit together in a circle. Slowly reveal each of the kitchen items. Stick the pictures in a line on the board. Divide the class into two teams and two lines. Give the first student in each line a flyswatter, call out a word, and the first student in each line runs and swats the correct flashcard. Switch to the next student in each line. If you don't have the flyswatters, students can touch the pictures instead.

> **Note to teachers**
> With big classes make three lines so students don't have to wait too long to have a turn.

### Watching the video – Let's watch!

### Materials and preparation
- Video library

Sit together and make sure all students can see the screen/board. Play *Nelly and Nora, Snow House* (video 15), and watch it together. Make sure to pause at the kitchen scene. Ask students what they can see. Allow them to use L1 as necessary. Together, do actions related to each kitchen item (e.g. wash the dishes at the sink, cook at the stove, etc.).
If necessary, play it again and ask students what the weather is like.
You should set expectations of correct watching behavior, reminding students that they should sit still and watch quietly, respecting their classmates.

### After watching the video – Look, think, and draw.

### Materials and preparation
- Colored pencils or crayons
- Project book page 23

Help students open their Project Books to page 23. Show students the picture with the empty refrigerator and empty cabinet. Point to each one and ask, *What can we draw in here?* Encourage them to share their ideas. Give students the pencils and crayons/colored pencils. Students draw things in the refrigerator and the cabinets.

> **Note to teachers**
> Support students by drawing some suggestions on the board. Students are unlikely to know the words in English. Support by telling them the words.

# DIFFERENTIATED INSTRUCTION

### BELOW LEVEL
### Before watching the video
Focus students' attention on the refrigerator and freezer only and mime opening it. Highlight the temperature difference and purpose.

### ABOVE LEVEL
### After watching the video
Ask students to draw other items in the kitchen.

# CLOSING

### Clean up the kitchen. Sing the *Goodbye song*.

### Materials and preparation
- Audio library – songs
- Boxes (to put the kitchen utensils)
- Plastic kitchen utensils (put them around the classroom)

Say, *Let's clean up the kitchen!* Encourage students to help each other to put away the kitchen utensils into the boxes. Sing the *Goodbye song* (track 5) and invite students to sing along. Say *goodbye* to them and have them say *goodbye* back to you.

**Learning goals**
- Develop motor skills and creativity
- Talk about different houses and places in the house.
- Give their opinion on a video

**Main language content**
Cold weather: *cold, freezer, igloo, snow*
*It's a house.*
*It's a snow house.*

# OPENING

## Circle time

### Materials and preparation
- Puppet
- Visual schedule pictures (hide them around the classroom)
- Weather chart and cards (optional)

Say, *Hello, how are you?* to the puppet and encourage students to greet it with *hello* or *hi*. Ask, *How are you?* Encourage them to answer (e.g. *I'm OK!*) and ask a classmate how they are. Ask students what the weather is like today. Mime *sunny*, *cloudy*, and *rainy* together.

> **Note to teachers**
> If you have a weather chart and cards available, you can invite a volunteer student to stick up the card for the weather.

Remind students of the attention-getter and practice it with them:
**T:** *Come and sit close to me. It's time for…*
**S:** *CBeebies!*
Or
**T:** *1, 2, 3! It's time for…*
**S:** *CBeebies!*

> **Note to teachers**
> Remind students that they should be quiet and pay attention when you use the attention-getter.

Hide the visual schedule pictures that refer to today's activities. Tell students to look for them around the classroom. As they find a picture, tell them to hand it to you. Then talk to students about each of the moments of the class.

### Where we live

**Materials and preparation**
- Pictures of castle house, houseboat, igloo, lighthouse, and tent

Sit together in a circle and show students the different houses. Ask students which ones are big and which ones are small. Stick the different pictures around the classroom. Divide the class into six groups and assign one pictures to each group. Students mime living in that house and then switch to the next house.

## ACTIVE LEARNING

### Before watching the video – It's cold!

**Materials and preparation**
- Pictures of cold weather, a freezer, an igloo, and snow
- Pictures of Inuit people (optional)

Sit together in a circle. Slow reveal each of the pictures. Mix them up, call out a word, and students point to the correct card. Together mime snowing, being cold, and building an igloo together.

> **Note to teachers**
> If available, show students pictures of Inuit people and talk about where they live.

### Watching the video – Let's watch!

**Materials and preparation**
- Video library

Sit together and make sure all students can see the screen/board. Play *Nelly and Nora, Snow House* (video 15), and watch it together. After the video, ask about the weather and what Nelly and Nora want to build. Ask, *How big is their igloo?* You should set expectations of correct watching behavior, reminding students that they should sit still and watch quietly, respecting their classmates.

### After watching the video – Make an igloo.

**Materials and preparation**
- Cotton balls
- Glue
- Sheets of A4 blue paper
- Rectangles of white paper (cut out, enough for students to make an igloo on a sheet of paper)

Ask students what shape blocks you need to build an igloo. Show students the rectangles of white paper and say, *rectangle*. Give students a sheet of blue paper and invite them to glue the white rectangles to build an igloo. Monitor and help as needed. Show students how to stick the cotton balls to make snow around the igloo.

> **Note to teachers**
> An alternative to this activity would be to ask students to build igloos using plastic boxes (like those used to store food) or plastic ice cubes. Try to use transparent plastic to give the idea of an ice block. This alterative could be done in small groups or pairs, depending on the size of the class and materials available. Hands-on play like this helps spark creativity.

## DIFFERENTIATED INSTRUCTION

### Below level
**Before watching the video**

Focus on familiar words (e.g. *castle, house, lighthouse*) and only introduce *igloo* as the new vocabulary. Reinforce these words during the *Before watching the video* task and focus less on the igloo type, structure, and temperature.

### ABOVE LEVEL
**After watching the video**

Once students have finished their igloo, put them into small groups and have them show, share, and describe their igloos. Monitor and help as needed.

## CLOSING

**Sing *Clean up time*. Sing the *Goodbye song*.**

**Materials and preparation**
- Audio library – songs

Sing *Clean up time* (track 11). Encourage students to help each other and to put the craft materials away properly while singing along.

Sing the *Goodbye song* (track 5) and invite students to sing along. Say *goodbye* to them and have them say *goodbye* back to you.

# Unit 6 How do you take care of pets?

### Learning goals
- Associate animals with their habitats
- Practice using words for body parts and size in context
- Use visuals to understand a video

### Main language content
Action: *walk*
Animals: *baby animals, elephant, giraffe*
Body parts: *ears, legs, neck, trunk*
Size: *big, long*

## OPENING

### Circle time

**Materials and preparation**
- A soft ball
- Audio library – songs
- Puppet
- Visual schedule pictures

Stand together in a circle and sing the *Hello song* (track 4). Give students the soft ball to pass on to other students and say, *hello*. Say, *Hello, how are you?* to the puppet and encourage students to do the same. Ask students what the weather is like today. Mime *sunny*, *cloudy*, and *rainy* together.

> **Note to teachers**
> If you have a weather chart and cards available, you can invite a volunteer student to stick up the card for the weather.

Remind students of the attention-getter and practice it with them:
**T:** *Come and sit close to me. It's time for…*
**S:** *CBeebies!*
Or
**T:** *1, 2, 3! It's time for…*
**S:** *CBeebies!*

Explain to students that whenever you use an attention-getter, they should stop talking and look at you.
Have students sit in a circle. Show students the visual schedule pictures. Ask for volunteers to help you turn them over. Encourage the whole class to say what each picture shows. Ask students to help you select the pictures that show today's schedule as you tell them what they are going to do today.

> **Note to teachers**
> You can also teach/review the attention-getter *All set? You bet!*

### Sing *Head, shoulders, knees, and toes*.

#### Materials and preparation
- Audio library – songs

Stand together in a circle and call out different body parts. Students listen and touch the correct body part. Sing *Head, shoulders, knees, and toes* (track 2) and do the actions together. Repeat to help students to remember and produce.

## ACTIVE LEARNING

### Before watching the video – Play *Animal statues*.

#### Materials and preparation
- Pictures of an elephant and a giraffe (or stuffed animals)

Sit together in a circle and slowly reveal the *elephant* and *giraffe* pictures (or stuffed animals). Stand up and mime each animal together. Ask students which animal has big ears, a long neck, a long trunk, and long legs. Have students answering by saying the words or simply pointing to the correct picture. Play the *Animal statues* game. Tell students to be an elephant and students mingle being elephants until you call out statues and everyone freezes. Repeat with *giraffe*.

#### Note to teachers
When you are describing the parts of the animal, mime and show students to aid understanding.

### Watching the video – Let's watch!

#### Materials and preparation
- Video library

Sit together and make sure all students can see the screen/board. Play *Andy's Baby Animals, Ep. 1, First Steps* (video 16), and watch it together. Play the video again and stop at each description of the body parts, repeat each word together. Stop and mime being the baby elephant wobbling along trying to walk. Encourage students to join in.
You should set expectations of correct watching behavior, reminding students that they should sit still and watch quietly, respecting their classmates.

### After watching the video – Look, think, draw, and match.

#### Materials and preparation
- Colored pencils and crayons
- Project Book page 25

Help students open their Project Books to page 25. Have students look at each body part in each circle. Ask students what they can see and what animal it is. Show students how match the body part with the animal.

#### Note to teachers
Encourage students to say the body parts as they match. Fast finishers can color the body parts.

## DIFFERENTIATED INSTRUCTION

### BELOW LEVEL
**Before watching the video**
Focus only on *long legs* and *big ears* and allow students to see and understand that distinction. Use the word *nose* instead of *trunk*.

### ABOVE LEVEL
**Before watching the video**
Focus on extended chunks of language, including *has*. For example, *The elephant has big ears*.

## CLOSING

### Act out being animals. Sing the *Goodbye song*.

#### Materials and preparation
- Audio library – songs
- Pictures of an elephant and a giraffe

Hold the pictures behind your back, one in each hand. Invite a student to choose a hand. Show the picture, making sure the other students can't see it. The students act out being that animal, and the other students have to say the name of the animal. Repeat with different students. Sing the *Goodbye song* (track 5). Say *goodbye* to students and have them say *goodbye* to you.

**Learning goals**
- Count to seven
- Develop motor skills in context
- Understand familiar words in a video

**Main language content**
Numbers: 1-7
How many (teddy bears) can you see?
Let's count!
I can see (two).

# OPENING

## Circle time

**Materials and preparation**
- A soft ball
- Puppet
- Visual schedule pictures

Say, *Hello, how are you?* to the puppet and encourage students to greet it with *hello* or *hi*. Have students sit in a circle. Roll the soft ball to a student and ask, *How are you?* Encourage them to answer (e.g. *I'm OK!*). Ask students what the weather is like today. Mime *sunny*, *cloudy*, and *rainy* together.

> **Note to teachers**
> If you have a weather chart and cards available, you can invite a volunteer student to stick up the card for the weather.

Remind students of the attention-getter and practice it with them:
**T:** *Come and sit close to me. It's time for…*
**S:** *CBeebies!*
Or
**T:** *1, 2, 3! It's time for…*
**S:** *CBeebies!*

> **Note to teachers**
> Remind students that they should be quiet and pay attention when you use the attention-getter.

Show them the visual schedule pictures. Choose a class helper of the day and have them order the pictures of the activities as they are mentioned.

**Count to seven.**

### Materials and preparation

- Small toys in groups of seven (at least two different toys – e.g. balls, cars, etc.)

Have students sit in a circle. Spread the toys in the center of the circle and sort out the different toys. Count together. Have students count again using their fingers.

# ACTIVE LEARNING

### Before watching the video – Put it in order.

### Materials and preparation

- Cards with the numbers 1-7

Stand together in a circle and count from one to seven on your fingers. Slowly reveal each of the number cards and have students say the numbers. Mix the cards up face up and invite students to come and put the numbers back in order. Then say the numbers together.

> **Note to teachers**
>
> Use things in class for students to count. Call out number *four* and students find four of something in the classroom.

### Watching the video – Let's watch!

### Materials and preparation

- Video library

Sit together and make sure everyone can see the screen/board. Play *Num Tums, Series 1, Ep. 7* (video 17), and watch it together. Play the video again, pause it to count aloud together. Air write number seven together.
You should set expectations of correct watching behavior, reminding students that they should sit still and watch quietly, respecting their classmates.

### After watching the video – Look, find, and stick.

### Materials and preparation

- Crayons
- Project Book page 27

Help students open their Project Books to page 27. Ask students to find the teddy bears, point to them, and count them. Help them turn to the stickers page, peel off the stickers, and stick them on the teddy bear outlines. Help them with the stickers as needed. Ask students to count them again, and then color the number 7.

# DIFFERENTIATED INSTRUCTION

### BELOW LEVEL
### Before watching the video

### Materials and preparation

- A box
- Seven balls

Use balls instead of showing the number cards. Count the balls together and invite students to count out balls from a box. Show the card numbers in order and have students repeat them.

### ABOVE LEVEL
### Before watching the video

Invite students to air write each of the numbers as you call them out and show the number cards.

# CLOSING

### Roll the die. Sing the *Goodbye song*.

### Materials and preparation

- A die (a large, foam die, if possible)
- Audio library – songs

Have students sit in a circle. Roll a die and have them count and say the number. Invite different students to roll the die and have all the class to say the number. Sing the *Goodbye song* (track 5). Say *goodbye* to students and have them say *goodbye* back to you.

**Learning goals**
- Count to seven
- Identify and classify animals
- Understand familiar words in a video

**Main language content**
Animals: *bear, elephant, giraffe, Guinea pig,*
Numbers: *1-7*
Toy: *teddy bear*
*How many (elephants) can you see?*
*Let's count!*

# OPENING

**Circle time**

**Materials and preparation**
- A soft ball
- Audio library – songs
- Puppet
- Visual schedule pictures

Stand together in a circle and sing the *Hello song* (track 4). Give students the soft ball to pass on to other students and say, *hello*. Say, *Hello, how are you?* to the puppet and encourage students to greet it with *hello* or *hi*. Ask students what the weather is like today. Mime *sunny, cloudy,* and *rainy* together.

> **Note to teachers**
> Start asking students how they feel about the weather. Ask, *Do you like (sunny/rainy/cloudy/windy) weather?*

Remind students of the attention-getter and practice it with them:
**T:** *Come and sit close to me. It's time for...*
**S:** *CBeebies!*
Or
**T:** *1, 2, 3! It's time for...*
**S:** *CBeebies!*

> **Note to teachers**
> You can also teach/review the attention-getter *All set? You bet!*

Have students sit in a circle. Show each visual schedule picture and then separate the ones that show the activities of today's class. Have a volunteer place the activities in the center of the circle.

**Count the animals.**

**Materials and preparation**
- Pictures of different animals in groups to count up to seven (e.g. one elephant, two giraffes, three bears, etc.)

Stand together in a circle and count from one to seven together on your fingers. Spread the pictures in the center of the circle. Have students sort out the animals and count together.

# ACTIVE LEARNING

**Before watching the video – Look, count, and say.**

**Materials and preparation**
- Cards with the numbers 1-7

Sit together in a circle and show students each card. Lay the numbers in order face up and tell students to close their eyes. Take away a random number in the sequence. Tell students to open their eyes and ask count together so that they notice there is a number missing. Ask, *What number is missing?*

> **Note to teachers**
> Invite the students to take away a number for the class to identify.

**Watching the video – Let's watch!**

**Materials and preparation**
- Video library

Sit together and make Play *Num Tums*, Series 1, Ep. 7 (video 17), and watch together. Stop to count each item as it comes up on the video.
You should set expectations of correct watching behavior, reminding students that they should sit still and watch quietly, respecting their classmates.

**After watching the video – Make a teddy bear mask.**

**Materials and preparation**
- Brown crayons (one per student)
- Brown crepe paper
- Glue
- Paper plates (one per student)
- Popsicle sticks (one per student)

Give each student a paper plate. Together, draw two big eyes on the plate and a big nose. Then color the plate brown and stick on two ears using crepe paper. Tell students it's a teddy bear mask. Stick on a popsicle stick.
When they have finished, get students to mingle together and then call out a number between one and seven. Students get into teddy bear groups of that number.

> **DIFFERENTIATED INSTRUCTION**
>
> **BELOW LEVEL**
> **Before watching the video**
> Show students the number cards in order and count together. Say one number and have students repeat after you.
>
> **ABOVE LEVEL**
> **After watching the video**
> Encourage students to tell you how many teddy bears there are in their mini-groups. e.g. *We are (five) teddy bears.*

# CLOSING

**Clap, count, and say. Sing the *Goodbye song*.**

**Materials and preparation**
- Audio library – songs

Have students sit in a circle. Clap once and have students say, *one*. Clap twice, and students say, *two*. Keep clapping and counting. Invite different students to clap so that their classmates say the number. Sing the *Goodbye song* (track 5), inviting students to sing along while they put things away. Encourage students to help each other. Say *goodbye* to them and have them say *goodbye* back to you.

**Learning goals**
- Recognize what a dog needs
- Understand that pets have needs and we need to take care of them
- Explain understanding of a video

**Main language content**
Pets: *cat, dog, fish, hamster*
Items for pets: *collar, food, leash, toy, water*
Action: *bark, play*
A *pet needs (food).*
*(He's) thirsty.*

# OPENING

### Circle time

#### Materials and preparation
- Puppet
- Visual schedule pictures (hide them around the classroom)
- Weather chart and cards (optional)

Say, *Hello, how are you?* to the puppet and encourage students to greet it with *hello* or *hi.* Ask, *How are you?* Encourage them to answer (e.g. *I'm OK!*) and ask a classmate how they are. Ask students what the weather is like today. Mime *sunny, cloudy,* and *rainy* together.

> **Note to teachers**
> If you have a weather chart and cards available, you can invite a volunteer student to stick up the card for the weather.

Remind students of the attention-getter and practice it with them:
**T:** *Come and sit close to me. It's time for…*
**S:** *CBeebies!*
Or
**T:** *1, 2, 3! It's time for…*
**S:** *CBeebies!*

> **Note to teachers**
> Remind students that they should be quiet and pay attention when you use the attention-getter.

Hide the visual schedule pictures that refer to today's activities. Tell students to look for them around the classroom. As they find a picture, tell them to hand it to you. Then talk to students about each of the moments of the class.

### Let's be pets!

#### Materials and preparation
- Flashcards: *cat, dog, hamster, fish*

Sit together in a circle. Slowly reveal each of the flashcards. Mime one of the animals for students to guess. Invite students to mime an animal for the class to guess. Stick the animals up around the room, call out an animal and students run to the card and mime and say it. You should set expectations of walking safely so as to avoid accidents.

## ACTIVE LEARNING

### Before watching the video – Items for pets

#### Materials and preparation
- Different items for pets: a collar, a leash, a toy, food, water, fishbowl, etc. (real items or pictures)
- Printouts: *cat, dog, hamster, fish*

Sit together in a circle and show students the pet objects and lay them out in the circle. Show them each of the flashcards. Ask students which pets need a collar, a leash, food, water, etc. Invite students to match the objects with the pets. Have them observe that all the pets need some of the items (e.g. *food, water,* etc.)

> **Note to teachers**
> Encourage students to say, *A (cat) needs food* and invite students to think of other things these pets need.

### Watching the video – Let's watch!

#### Materials and preparation
- Video library

Sit together and make sure everyone can see the screen/board. Play *Nelly and Nora, Ep. 25, Hot Dog* (video 18), and watch together. Pause to ask students what the dog needs and why. Stop and ask students what other things they recognize in the video. You should set expectations of correct watching behavior, reminding students that they should sit still and watch quietly, respecting their classmates.

### After watching the video – Make a doggy card.

#### Materials and preparation
- A4 sheets of card (one per student)
- Colored pencils or crayons
- Crepe paper
- Glue
- Scissors
- Wool or string

Give students the art supplies and a sheet of card. Show students how to fold the two sides into the center. Open up the side flaps and inside draw a dog together. Ask students what the dog needs and use the wool or string to make a leash and collar and stick it on the dog. Use the crepe paper or card to make a water and food bowl.

> **Note to teachers**
> At this age, students will not be able to draw a perfect, or even a detailed dog. This activity stimulates their creativity; as they are drawing ask them to tell you about the dog they are drawing.

## DIFFERENTIATED INSTRUCTION

### Below level
### Before watching the video

Focus only on the *dog* and mime being a dog together. Highlight that dogs bark and how they play by chasing. Play statues together, where students run around being dogs and freeze when you say *statues*.

### Above level
### After watching the video

When students have finished, put them into groups with their craft. Together students show and share their doggy cards and say what the dogs need.

## CLOSING

### Sing *Why is that doggie in the window?* Sing the *Goodbye song*.

#### Materials and preparation
- Audio library – songs

Sing *Why is that doggie in the window?* (track 21) and encourage students to sing along. Sing the *Goodbye song* (track 5) and invite students to sing along while they help you clean up the classroom. Say *goodbye* to them and have them say *goodbye* back to you.

# Unit 7 What's your favorite food?

**Learning goals**
- Learn about different types of food
- Understand about what a fruit is
- Understand familiar words in a video

**Main language content**
Colors
Fruits: *apple, banana, orange, watermelon*
Nature: *seeds, plants,*
Places in town: *supermarket*
*I want (two) (apples).*

## OPENING

**Circle time**

**Materials and preparation**
- A soft ball
- Audio library – songs
- Puppet
- Visual schedule pictures

Stand together in a circle and sing the *Hello song* (track 4). Give students the soft ball to pass on to other students and say, *hello*. Say, *Hello, how are you?* to the puppet and encourage students to do the same. Ask students what the weather is like today and if they like it.

> **Note to teachers**
> Encourage students to express their feelings on the weather, telling you if they like or don't like the weather.

Remind students of the attention-getter and practice it with them:
**T:** *Come and sit close to me. It's time for…*
**S:** *CBeebies!*
Or
**T:** *1, 2, 3! It's time for…*
**S:** *CBeebies!*
Explain to students that whenever you use an attention-getter, they should stop talking and look at you.
Have students sit in a circle. Show students the visual schedule pictures. Ask for volunteers to help you turn them over. Encourage the whole class to say what each picture shows. Ask students to help you select the pictures that show today's schedule as you tell them what they are going to do today.

> **Note to teachers**
> You can also teach/review the attention-getter *All set? You bet!*

### Sing *It's getting late.*

**Materials and preparation**

- Audio library – songs

Sing *It's getting late* (track 18). Have students sing along and join in with the actions.

# ACTIVE LEARNING

### Before watching the video – Listen and draw.

**Materials and preparation**

- Crayons
- Pictures of apples, bananas, oranges, watermelons (or plastic fruits), a plant, seeds (or a real plant and seeds)
- Sheets of A4 paper (one per student)

Sit together in a circle and show students the picture of a plant (or a real plant). Ask students what grows on plants. Slow reveal the pictures of the fruits (or plastic fruits) and tell students fruit grow on plants. Show students the *seed* picture (or real seeds) and help them understand that plants and fruits grow from seeds.

Give each student a sheet of paper and crayons. Help them divide the page into two parts. Tell students to listen and draw. Say, *three apples* and have them draw the apples. The say, *two bananas* and have them draw. Ask, *How many fruits are there? What color are they?*

> **Note to teachers**
> Make sure you allow only a short time for the drawing.

### Watching the video – Let's watch!

**Materials and preparation**

- Video library

Sit together and make sure all students can see the screen/board. Play the video *Kit & Pup, Ep. 47, Fruit* (video 19), and watch it together. Play the video again and stop to ask students what fruit they can see, where it is and what colors they can see. Count the fruits together.

You should set expectations of correct watching behavior, reminding students that they should sit still and watch quietly, respecting their classmates.

### After watching the video – Grocery store role-play

**Materials and preparation**

- Pictures of apples, bananas, watermelons, oranges (or plastic/real fruits)
- Small reusable bags

Set up two or three tables with fruits laid out. Model the task by inviting a student to stand behind the table while you act as the customer. Ask for fruit using *I want (two) (apples)*.

Organize the class into two or three groups and each group into customers and storeowners. The customers ask for fruit, and the storeowners give them the fruit in small bags. Switch roles so every student gets the chance at both roles.

> **Note to teachers**
> You can use plastic or real fruit for students to use in the role-play. If there's time, make a craft basket together for students to put their fruits in.

# DIFFERENTIATED INSTRUCTION

**BELOW LEVEL**
**After watching the video**

Students don't need to say the full phrase and can just point at the fruit.

**ABOVE LEVEL**
**After watching the video**

Students can draw a shopping list of the items they want before the role-play and can include other fruit they know.

# CLOSING

### Give me some juice. Sing the *Goodbye song.*

**Materials and preparation**

- Audio library – songs

Pretend to be thirsty, draw a glass on the board, and say, *I want some juice*. Encourage students to say what fruit juice you can drink, and what is their favorite fruit juice.

Sing the *Goodbye song* (track 5). Say *goodbye* to students and have them say *goodbye* back to you.

**Learning goals**
- Express preference about fruits
- Learn about different types of food
- Give their opinion on a video

**Main language content**
Fruits: *apple, banana, orange, pineapple, watermelon*
School item: *lunchbox*
*I like (apples).*
*I don't like (apples).*

# OPENING

**Circle time**

**Materials and preparation**
- A soft ball
- Puppet
- Visual schedule pictures

Say, *Hello, how are you?* to the puppet and encourage students to greet it with *hello* or *hi*. Have students sit in a circle. Roll the soft ball to a student and ask, *How are you?* Encourage them to answer (e.g. *I'm OK!*). Ask students what the weather is like today. Mime *sunny, cloudy,* and *rainy* together.

> **Note to teachers**
> If you have a weather chart and cards available, you can invite a volunteer student to stick up the card for the weather.

Remind students of the attention-getter and practice it with them:
**T:** *Come and sit close to me. It's time for...*
**S:** *CBeebies!*
Or
**T:** *1, 2, 3! It's time for...*
**S:** *CBeebies!*

> **Note to teachers**
> Remind students that they should be quiet and pay attention when you use the attention-getter.

Show them the visual schedule pictures. Choose a class helper of the day and have them order the pictures of the activities as they are mentioned.

**Counting fruits**

**Materials and preparation**
- A song or video counting fruits (easily found online – search for "counting fruits." or any other fruit songs)

Play the song and invite students to join in singing and counting. Encourage them to count the fruits and draw the fruits on the board to help them count.

# ACTIVE LEARNING

### Before watching the video – I like it!

**Materials and preparation**
- Pictures of apples, bananas, oranges, pineapples, and watermelons

Sit together in a circle and show each picture. Lay the pictures face down in the center of the circle, mix them up, call out a fruit, and invite a student to try to find the correct fruit.
Pick up a fruit picture, make a happy face, and say, *I like (fruit)*. Repeat with, *I don't like (fruit)*. Invite students to show you the fruit they like and don't like.

> **Note to teachers**
> Students are not expected to produce the full sentence. Exposure and concept understanding are more important at this point.

### Watching the video – Let's watch!

**Materials and preparation**
- Video library

Sit together and make sure all students can see the screen/board. Play the video *Kit & Pup, Ep. 47, Fruit* (video 19), and watch it together. Play it again and stop the video to ask students what fruit they can see, what colors they are, the number of fruits they can count. At the end, ask if they like or don't like the fruit they can see in the video.
You should set expectations of correct watching behavior, reminding students that they should sit still and watch quietly, respecting their classmates.

### After watching the video – What's in my lunchbox?

**Materials and preparation**
- A large, children's lunchbox (or a shoe box with a lid)
- Colored pencils
- Plastic/toy fruits (as much as possible, try to include other foods if possible)
- Sheets of paper

Place a selection of the plastic food into a lunchbox/box with a lid. Sit with students in a circle. Show the box and say, *It's my lunchbox! What's in my lunchbox?* Encourage them to guess. Pass the lunchbox around, inviting students to take turns opening it, and taking out the food. Encourage them to say the words. When everyone has participated, place the food in the center of the circle. Give volunteer students the lunchbox and invite them to choose two or three items to put in their lunchboxes. Encourage them to say what they are choosing. Then give students the sheets of paper and pencils, and invite them to draw their lunchbox with their lunch in it.

> **Note to teachers**
> The exact shape of the fruits is less important as long students are clear on the color and what fruit they think they have created.

# DIFFERENTIATED INSTRUCTION

**BELOW LEVEL**
**Before watching the video**
Focus only on *I like (fruit)* and emphasize using lots of mime and gestures. Stick the fruit cards up around the room and together go to each card and say, *I like (fruit)*, lick your lips, and say, *yummy, yummy* all together.

**ABOVE LEVEL**
**After watching the video**
Allow students to freely choose what fruit and how many of each to put in their lunchbox drawings.

# CLOSING

### Show and tell. Sing the *Goodbye song*.

**Materials and preparation**
- Audio library – songs

Invite students to share their lunchboxes with each other, show and tell what fruits they drew.
Sing the *Goodbye song* (track 5). Say *goodbye* to them and have them say *goodbye* back to you.

## OPENING

### Circle time

**Materials and preparation**
- A soft ball
- Audio library – songs
- Puppet
- Visual schedule pictures

Stand together in a circle and sing the *Hello song* (track 4). Give students the soft ball to pass on to other students and say, *hello*. Say, *Hello, how are you?* to the puppet and encourage students to greet it with *hello* or *hi*. Ask students what the weather is like today. Mime *sunny*, *cloudy*, and *rainy* together.

> **Note to teachers**
> Encourage students to express their feelings on the weather, telling you if they like or don't like the weather.

Remind students of the attention-getter and practice it with them:
**T:** *Come and sit close to me. It's time for…*
**S:** *CBeebies!*
Or
**T:** *1, 2, 3! It's time for…*
**S:** *CBeebies!*

> **Note to teachers**
> You can also teach/review the attention-getter *All set? You bet!*

Have students sit in a circle. Show each visual schedule picture and then separate the ones that show the activities of today's class. Have a volunteer place the activities in the center of the circle.

**Learning goals**
- Count to nine
- Develop motor skills in context
- Understand familiar words in a video

**Main language content**
Numbers: 1-9
*How many (balls) can you see?*
*Let's count.*
*I can see (balls/flowers/robots).*

### Count to nine.

**Materials and preparation**
- Nine balls (different colors, if possible) in a box

Stand together in a circle. Count to nine together using your fingers. Sit down in a circle. Pull out a ball from the box and count together until nine. Put the ball back in the box. Call out a number between one and nine and invite a student to come to the box and count out the right number of balls. Repeat to allow as many students as possible to try.

## ACTIVE LEARNING

### Before watching the video – Number sequence

**Materials and preparation**
- Cards with the numbers 1–9 (one number on each card)

Sit together in a circle and slow reveal each of the number cards. Put the cards face down, mix up the cards, and invite students to sequence the numbers starting with finding number 1 up to number 9.

> **Note to teachers**
> For large classes you can use sets of mini-cards and get students to work together in small groups.

### Watching the video – Let's watch!

**Materials and preparation**
- Video library

Sit together and make Play the video *Num Tums, Series 1, Ep. 9* (video 20), and watch it together. Play it again and stop to count the items together in the video. Focus on *ball*, *flower*, and *robot*.
You should set expectations of correct watching behavior, reminding students that they should sit still and watch quietly, respecting their classmates.

### After watching the video – Look, think, and draw.

**Materials and preparation**
- Crayons
- Pencils
- Project Book page 29

Help students open their Project Books to page 29. Count the robots together. Students trace the outline of each robot with a pencil and count the robots as they trace. Then they color the robots. Encourage them to color each robot in a different way. Finally, they color the number 9.

> **Note to teachers**
> At the end, air write number nine together with students.

## DIFFERENTIATED INSTRUCTION

### BELOW LEVEL
**Before watching the video**

Call out the numbers in sequence, rather than random order and invite students to find the correct number of balls.

### ABOVE LEVEL
**Before watching the video**

Stick the number cards on the back of nine students, without those students seeing what number they are. Invite the rest of the class to put them in sequence from 1 to 9 and then ask each student what number is on their back. Switch around so every student has a turn.

## CLOSING

### Look and say. Sing the *Goodbye song*.

**Materials and preparation**
- Audio library – songs

Have students sit in a circle. Air write a number slowly and encourage students to which number it is. Repeat with another number if you have time and encourage students to repeat the action with you. Sing the *Goodbye song* (track 5) and invite students to sing along while they clean up and put their things away. Encourage students to help each other. Say *goodbye* to them and have them say *goodbye* back to you.

**LOOK, FIND, AND DRAW.**

CBEEBIES • WHAT'S YOUR FAVORITE FOOD? • UNIT 7   31

**Learning goals**
- Learn and practice words for farm food
- Understand a story about food
- Explain understanding of a story in a video

**Main language content**
Fruits and vegetables: *apples, carrots, corn, potatoes, pumpkin*
On the farm: costume, *farm, farmer, feast, harvest,*

# OPENING

**Circle time**

**Materials and preparation**
- A soft ball
- Audio library – songs
- Puppet
- Visual schedule pictures

Stand together in a circle and sing the *Hello song* (track 4). Give students the soft ball to pass on to other students and say, *hello*. Say, *Hello, how are you?* to the puppet and encourage students to greet it with *hello* or *hi*.
Remind students of the attention-getter and practice it with them:
**T:** *Come and sit close to me. It's time for...*
**S:** *Cbeebies!*
Or
**T:** *1, 2, 3! It's time for...*
**S:** *Cbeebies!*

> **Note to teachers**
> You can also teach/review the attention-getter *All set? You bet!*

### I like fruit!

**Materials and preparation**

- Large hula hoops (at least six)
- Pictures (or real/plastic food): apples, bananas, pineapple, watermelon, oranges, grapes

Show the pictures/fruits one by one. Ask, *What's this?* and help students say the words. Lay the hula hoops on the floor and picture a picture/fruit in each one. Ask for a volunteer student and say the name of the fruit. The student has to go to that hula hoop and stand it in. Then ask, *Do you like (apples)?* If they like the fruit, they stay inside the hula hoop. If not, they take a step outside of it. Then repeat with different students and fruits. You should set expectations of walking safely so as to avoid accidents.

## ACTIVE LEARNING

### Before watching the video

**Materials and preparation**

- Printouts: farmer, corn, pumpkin, potatoes, carrots, apples

Sit together in a circle and slow reveal each of the printouts. Mix up the pictures face-down and call out a word for students to find. Invite different students to find the picture, and encourage them to say the word as they identify it.

### Watching the video – Let's watch!

**Materials and preparation**

- Video library

Sit together in a circle and make sure all students can see the screen/board. Play the video *Nelly & Nora, Ep. 51, Harvest Feast* (video 21) and watch it together. Make sure to stop and ask, *What food can you see in the farmer's field?* Then pause and ask what you need for a harvest feast. Finally pause and ask what costumes students can see.

### After watching the video – Look, find, and draw.

**Materials and preparation**

- Colored pencils
- Pencil
- Project Book page 31

Help students open their Project Books to page 31. Ask, *What food can you see?* Encourage them to point to the different items and say the words. Give each student a pencil and put the colored pencils in the center of the table. Students find, trace, and color the food in the field.

> **Note to teachers**
>
> Walk around monitoring and asking students to say which food they like and don't like.

## DIFFERENTIATED INSTRUCTION

**BELOW LEVEL**
**I like fruit!**

Encourage students to answer *yes* or *no* when you ask them if they like the fruit.

**ABOVE LEVEL**
**I like fruit!**

Encourage students to answer using full sentences, *I like (apples)* or *I don't like (watermelon)*.

## CLOSING

### Sing the *Goodbye song*.

**Materials and preparation**

- Audio library – songs

Sit together with students in a circle. Tell them, *We are going to have a harvest feast. What are you going to bring?* Invite each student to say what he/she would bring to a harvest feast.

Sing the *Goodbye* song (track 5) and invite students to sing along. Say *goodbye* to them and have them say *goodbye* back to you.

# Unit 8 What do you like about school?

**Learning goals**
- Develop creative and motor skills in context
- Learn about classroom objects
- Use visuals to understand a video

**Main language content**
School items: *backpack, book, chair, eraser, mini-book, pencil, table*
*This is my (book).*

## OPENING

**Circle time**

**Materials and preparation**
- A soft ball
- Audio library – songs
- Puppet
- Visual schedule pictures

Stand together in a circle and sing the *Hello song* (track 4). Give students the soft ball to pass on to other students and say, *hello*. Say, *Hello, how are you?* to the puppet and encourage students to do the same. Ask students what the weather is like today. Mime *sunny*, *cloudy*, and *rainy* together.

> **Note to teachers**
> If you have a weather chart and cards available, you can invite a volunteer student to stick up the card for the weather.

Remind students of the attention-getter and practice it with them:
**T:** *Come and sit close to me. It's time for…*
**S:** *CBeebies!*
Or
**T:** *1, 2, 3! It's time for…*
**S:** *CBeebies!*
Explain to students that whenever you use an attention-getter, they should stop talking and look at you.
Have students sit in a circle. Show students the visual schedule pictures. Ask for volunteers to help you turn them over. Encourage the whole class to say what each picture shows. Ask students to help you select the pictures that show today's schedule as you tell them what they are going to do today.

> **Note to teachers**
> You can also teach/review the attention-getter *All set? You bet!*

64  CBeebies

### In my classroom

#### Materials and preparation
- Pictures of a backpack, a book, a chair, an eraser, a pencil, a table

Slow reveal each of the school pictures. Stick the pictures around the classroom, stand together in the center, call out a classroom object, and students run to the correct picture. You should set expectations of walking safely as to avoid accidents.

## ACTIVE LEARNING

### Before watching the video – What's missing?

#### Materials and preparation
- Pictures of a backpack, a book, a chair, an eraser, a pencil, a table

Sit together in a circle and lay the cards out in a line in front of the class. Ask students to close their eyes; you take away a card. Students open their eyes and tell you what card is missing.

> **Note to teachers**
> Before asking students to close their eyes, say the whole sequence of words together several times to help students remember the words and the order.

### Watching the video – Let's watch!

#### Materials and preparation
- Video library

Sit together and make sure all students can see the screen/board. Play the video *Yakka Dee, Series 1, Ep. 3, Book* (video 22), and watch it together. Play it again and stop each time there is a book. Students say the word *book* and mime opening, reading, and closing a book.
You should set expectations of correct watching behavior, reminding students that they should sit still and watch quietly, respecting their classmates.

### After watching the video – Make a mini-book.

#### Materials and preparation
- Sheets of A4 paper (one per student)
- Colored pencils and crayons

Give each student a sheet of paper. Together fold it to make a mini-book. Tell students it's their mini-book with their favorite school thing. Ask students to choose one things to draw: a pencil, an eraser, a chair, a table, or a backpack. Alternatively, you can say to students what to draw. Have them decorate the cover of their mini-books.

## DIFFERENTIATED INSTRUCTION

### BELOW LEVEL
**Before watching the video**

Focus only on these three items *pencil*, *eraser*, and *book*. Work together on recognition on these three items, playing run and touch.

### AFTER LEVEL
**After watching the video**

#### Materials and preparation
- Sheets of A4 paper (one per student)
- Sticky tape

Give students more sheets of paper to create other pages for their mini-books. Help them fold and stick the pages for them using sticky tape.

## CLOSING

### Look around and count. Sing the *Goodbye song*.

#### Materials and preparation
- Audio library – songs

Invite students to look at their tables and around the classroom, identify the items, and count them.
Sing the *Goodbye song* (track 5) and invite students to sing along while they clean up and put their things away. Encourage students to help each other. Say *goodbye* to them and have them say *goodbye* back to you. Students can take their mini-books home to show to their families.

**CIRCLE, COUNT, AND CHECK.**

**Learning goals**
- Count to ten
- Recognize numbers up to ten in context
- Understand familiar words in a video

**Main language content**
Numbers: *1-10*
*How many (buttons) can you see?*
*Let's count.*
*I can see (buttons).*

# OPENING

## Circle time

### Materials and preparation
- A soft ball
- Puppet
- Visual schedule pictures

Say, *Hello, how are you?* to the puppet and encourage students to greet it with *hello* or *hi*. Have students sit in a circle. Roll the soft ball to a student and ask, *How are you?* Encourage them to answer (e.g. *I'm OK!*). Ask students what the weather is like today. Mime *sunny*, *cloudy*, and *rainy* together.

> **Note to teachers**
> If you have a weather chart and cards available, you can invite a volunteer student to stick up the card for the weather.

Remind students of the attention-getter and practice it with them:
**T:** *Come and sit close to me. It's time for...*
**S:** *CBeebies!*
Or
**T:** *1, 2, 3! It's time for...*
**S:** *CBeebies!*

> **Note to teachers**
> Remind students that they should be quiet and pay attention when you use the attention-getter.

Show them the visual schedule pictures. Choose a class helper of the day and have them order the pictures of the activities as they are mentioned.

### Sing the *School* song.

**Materials and preparation**
- Audio library – songs

Sing the *School* song (track 19) and have students sing and dance along. Stop the music and encourage them to keep singing and dancing.
Ask them to count to look around and count up to ten (e.g. five books, nine pencils, ten backpacks, etc.).

## ACTIVE LEARNING

### Before watching the video – Touch the number.

**Materials and preparation**
- Number cards: 1-10
- Two flyswatters (optional)

Sit together in a circle. Slowly reveal each of the numbers. Stick the numbers on the board in sequence and get students into two groups and two lines. Give the first student in each line a flyswatter (if available), call out a number, and students race and swat. Those students pass on the flyswatter to the next person in the line to have a turn. Continue until everyone has a turn. If you don't have the flyswatters, students can simply touch the cards.
You should set expectations of walking safely so as to avoid accidents.

**Note to teachers**
For large classes divide the class into three groups so students don't have to wait too long to have their turn.

### Watching the video – Let's watch!

**Materials and preparation**
- Video library

Sit together and make sure all students can see the screen/board. Play the video *Num Tums, Series 1, Ep. 10* (video 23), and watch it together. Play the video again and count the butterflies, candies, and buttons together.
You should set expectations of correct watching behavior, reminding students that they should sit still and watch quietly, respecting their classmates.

### After watching the video – Circle, count, and check.

**Materials and preparation**
- Colored pencils or crayons
- Project Book page 33

Help students open their Project Books to page 33. Ask, *What can you see?* and encourage students to describe the page. Then point to the small pictures in the chart and elicit the words. Ask students to find the first picture in the main picture and circle them. Then ask them to count how many they circled. Students draw a checkmark in the chart if there are 10 of that object.

**Note to teachers**
Together air write the number ten.

## DIFFERENTIATED INSTRUCTION

### BELOW LEVEL
**Before watching the video**
Get students to work in pairs to run and swat the correct number. This will help *below level* students and make the activity more collaborative.

### ABOVE LEVEL
**After watching the video**

**Materials and preparation**
- Scissors
- Sheets of colored paper

Students draw a big circle. Help them cut it out to make a big button. On the back, students write the number ten.

## CLOSING

### Count the buttons. Sing the *Goodbye* song.

**Materials and preparation**
- A bag filled with several buttons (make sure these aren't too small)
- Audio library – songs

Have students sit in a circle, close their eyes, and hold out their hands. Walk around giving students a number of buttons. As soon as they feel you place the buttons in their hand, they close it shut. When you've given buttons to all of the students, tell them to open their eyes, look in their hands, and count the buttons. Ask them to share how much buttons they have with the rest of the class.

**Note to teachers**
Give more buttons to students who are more confident saying higher numbers, give less buttons to students who are more confident only with numbers one to five.

Sing the *Goodbye song* (track 5). Say *goodbye* to students and have them say *goodbye* back to you.

**Learning goals**
- Count to ten
- Develop creative and motor skills in context
- Understand familiar words in a video

**Main language content**
Miscellaneous: *butterflies, buttons, candies, giraffes*
Numbers: *1-10*
*How many (buttons) can you see?*
*Let's count. I can see (three).*

# OPENING

## Circle time

**Materials and preparation**
- A soft ball
- Audio library – songs
- Puppet
- Visual schedule pictures

Stand together in a circle and sing the *Hello song* (track 4). Give students the soft ball to pass on to other students and say, *hello*. Say, *Hello, how are you?* to the puppet and encourage students to greet it with *hello* or *hi*. Ask students what the weather is like today. Mime *sunny, cloudy,* and *rainy* together.

> **Note to teachers**
> If you have a weather chart and cards available, you can invite a volunteer student to stick up the card for the weather.

Remind students of the attention-getter and practice it with them:
**T:** *Come and sit close to me. It's time for…*
**S:** *CBeebies!*
Or
**T:** *1, 2, 3! It's time for…*
**S:** *CBeebies!*

> **Note to teachers**
> You can also teach/review the attention-getter *All set? You bet!*

Have students sit in a circle. Show each visual schedule picture and then separate the ones that show the activities of today's class. Have a volunteer place the activities in the center of the circle.

**Sing *If you're happy and you know it*.**

### Materials and preparation
- Audio library – songs

Sing *If you're happy and you know it* (track 7) and encourage students to sing along and join in with the actions.
Clap your hands together counting to ten. Then repeat counting, but this time stomping your feet.

# ACTIVE LEARNING

**Before watching the video – Count the balls.**

### Materials and preparation
- A box with 10 balls
- Number cards: 1-10

Sit together in a circle and slow reveal the numbers from one to ten. Turn the cards over face down and mix up the cards. Call out a number and students try to find the number. Put the box of balls in the center of the circle, invite students to pick a number card randomly, say the number, and count out the right amount of balls from the box.

> **Note to teachers**
> As students count out the number of balls, encourage all the class to count along to support and practice.

**Watching the video – Let's watch!**

### Materials and preparation
- Video library

Sit together and make sure all students can see the screen/board. Play the video *Num Tums, Series 1, Ep. 10* (video 23), and watch it together. Play the video again and stop to count each of the objects in the video. Count out on your fingers to help students remember the numbers.
You should set expectations of correct watching behavior, reminding students that they should sit still and watch quietly, respecting their classmates.

**After watching the video – Make a chain of candies.**

### Materials and preparation
- Crepe paper
- Glue
- Small card circles
- String or ribbon

Take a small card circle and two small pieces of crepe paper. Scrunch up the ends and stick them opposite each other on the circle to make a candy. Divide students into groups of four and ask them to try to make ten candies. Give students the string or ribbon to stick the ten candies.

> **Note to teachers**
> Play the *Ten in the bed* song (easily found online; or any other song for numbers 1-10) while students make their candies to keep students focused and on track.

# DIFFERENTIATED INSTRUCTION

## BELOW LEVEL
**Before watching the video**

Lay the number cards out in sequence for all students to see. Invite students to take out the right amount of balls and put them next to the number card in sequence. Doing this in sequence rather than randomly will support lower level students.

## ABOVE LEVEL
**After watching the video**

### Materials and preparation
- Soft tip colored markers

Students practice number formation by air writing each number and then try out writing the number on the back of each candy in the chain. Students can use a soft tip marker pen.

# CLOSING

**Share the candies. Sing the *Goodbye song*.**

### Materials and preparation
- A large number of individually wrapped candies
- Audio library – songs
- Stuffed animals

Place the stuffed animals and the candies in the middle of the circle and point to the center. Tell students that the animals have a lot of candies! You could ask them to speculate on why they have so many candies, thinking about when they themselves get given a lot of candy, e.g. on a special holiday. Invite students to help you share the candies among the stuffed animals.
Then you can invite students to take one candy each for themselves. We recommend you choose some healthier choices of candies and check if your students don't have any allergies. Praise students on sharing and only taking their share.
Sing the *Goodbye song* (track 5). Say *goodbye* to students and have them say *goodbye* back to you.

Unit 8 | 69

# OPENING

## Circle time

### Materials and preparation
- Puppet
- Visual schedule pictures (hide them around the classroom)

Say, *Hello, how are you?* to the puppet and encourage students to greet it with *hello* or *hi*. Ask, *How are you?* Encourage them to answer (e.g. *I'm OK!*) and ask a classmate how they are.

Remind students of the attention-getter and practice it with them:
**T:** *Come and sit close to me. It's time for…*
**S:** *CBeebies!*
Or
**T:** *1, 2, 3! It's time for…*
**S:** *CBeebies!*

> **Note to teachers**
> Remind students that they should be quiet and pay attention when you use the attention-getter.

Hide the visual schedule pictures that refer to today's activities. Tell students to look for them around the classroom. As they find a picture, tell them to hand it to you. Then talk to students about each of the moments of the class.

## Play the *Prepositions game*.

### Materials and preparation
- Classroom items: a backpack, a book, an eraser, and a pencil

Sit students at their tables and show students each of the classroom objects. Put the pencil *on* the table, the book *under* a chair, the bag *behind* the door, and the eraser *in* the bin. Highlight the prepositions of place. Invite students to put the items *in*, *on*, *under*, and *behind* different objects in the class for the other students to say.

## Learning goals
- Ask and answer what and where something is
- Recognize prepositions of place
- Explain understanding of a video

## Main language content
Prepositions: *in, on, under, behind*
*Let's look for (the cat).*

# ACTIVE LEARNING

### Before watching the video – Let's look for the cat!

#### Materials and preparation
- Pictures of a box, cat, house, table, tree branch
- Sticky tack

Sit together in a circle. Slowly reveal each of the pictures. Stick the table, house, box, and tree branch on the board. Tell students, *Let's look for the cat*. Instruct students that the cat is under the table and invite a student to take the picture of the cat and stick it under the table on the board. Continue changing the objects and prepositions of place.

> **Note to teachers**
> To make this more inclusive and interactive, prepare a set of mini-pictures/cards for students to use in pairs or small groups.

### Watching the video

#### Materials and preparation
- Video library – Nora and Nelly, Ep. 20, Moon Path

Sit together in a circle and make sure all students can see. Play the video *Nora and Nelly, Ep. 20, Moon Path* (video 24), and watch it together. Watch the video again and ask students, *Where are Nora and Nelly looking for the cat?* Ask students to mime together following the moon path. At the end, ask, *Where is the cat now?* You should set expectations of correct watching behavior, reminding students that they should sit still and watch quietly, respecting their classmates.

### After watching the video – Look, think, and stick.

#### Materials and preparation
- Colored pencils or crayons
- Project Book page 35

Help students open their Project Books to page 35. Ask, *What can you see?* Help them turn to the stickers page at the back of the book. Help them with the stickers as needed. Ask students where the cat is in each place. Students look, match, and stick the stickers.

> **Note to teachers**
> Fast finishers can color the places where the cat is.

# DIFFERENTIATED INSTRUCTION

### Below level
### After watching the video
Scaffold the task completely by doing each sticker together and using the flashcards on the board to show students exactly where the cat is in each place.

### Above level
### After watching the video
Invite students to think of another animal to draw next to the cat in each place. Divide students into groups to show, share, and say what animal they have and where.

# CLOSING

### Sing *Clean up time*. Sing the *Goodbye song*.

#### Materials and preparation
- Audio library – songs

Sing the *Clean up time* (track 11) song. Encourage students to help each put their things away and get ready to go.
Sing the *Goodbye song* (track 5) and invite students to sing along. Say *goodbye* to them and have them say *goodbye* back to you.

# Notes

# Notes

# Notes

# Notes

# Notes

# Notes

# Notes

# Notes

# Notes